Linguistics *in* Philosophy

LINGUISTICS
IN
PHILOSOPHY

Zeno Vendler

Cornell University Press

Ithaca and London

First published 1967 by Cornell University Press.
Fourth printing 1979

Published in the United Kingdom by Cornell University Press Ltd., 2-4 Brook Street, London W1Y1 1AA

International Standard Book Number 0-8014-0436-3
Library of Congress Catalog Card Number 67-18221

Printed in the United States of America

For Semiramis

Preface

This work is a progress report. It contains seven essays representing the gradual introduction of a new technique into analytic philosophy. The emergence of this method, to my mind, is nothing but the natural continuation of the line of development that goes through the philosophers of ordinary language to J. L. Austin. Along this line the appeal to the facts of our natural language, which is the common feature of this whole approach, becomes more and more systematic. The philosophers of ordinary language used these facts as they found them and as they needed them for their various purposes in an intuitive fashion. Austin tried to organize these facts according to principles of his own invention. The present method consists in an appeal to the facts of language already organized by the science of structural linguistics.

The essays in this book were written in the years between 1956 and 1965. During this period, to be exact from 1952 on, structural linguistics itself was revolutionized through the development of transformational analysis.

My acquaintance with this method goes back only to 1959. Two essays (contained in Chapters 3 and 4) had been completed before that time, and the remaining five (contained in Chapters 6, 7, 5, 1, and 2, in the order of their composition) mirror the growth of the underlying linguistic theory. Each new insight into the syntactical structure of the language is bound to have repercussions beyond the immediate field of the discovery. Accordingly, I now feel that the earlier papers could be rewritten with profit and all of them integrated into a more coherent whole. I decided against doing this for two reasons. In the first place, the development of transformational grammar is by no means complete, and I have no reason to think that its present state will be permanent even for a short period of time. The second reason is that the earlier material, in spite of its many imperfections, has become known among a number of philosophers, so that it would be unfair to ask them to follow me in my present wanderings over the same terrain. The point of this work is not to offer impeccable solutions for a few problems, but to show that the more or less sophisticated data provided by structural linguistics can be used in philosophical arguments. Even if better data in more capable hands should override some of my conclusions, this work will have achieved its aim. Thus I have restricted my revisions to passages in which I had been clearly wrong, and I did not press unity beyond the point of conceptual and terminological consistency.

The material making up four of the seven chapters (3, 4, 6, 7) has been published before. According to what I just said, in spite of the several corrections, insertions, and occasional rewriting, I tried to preserve the original papers substantially the same. Bibliographical data are given in the text.

I have kept the technical apparatus to a necessary minimum. The text does not require any previous acquaintance with transformational grammar, and the only symbols I have used in giving transformations are very elementary: *N* for noun, *A* for adjective, *V* for verb, *D* for adverb, *P* for preposition. In exhibiting words, phrases, or sentences I conform to the style of the linguists by italicizing them rather than giving them in quotation marks. The asterisk (*) in front marks deviant sentences. A technical account of the grammatical background behind Chapters 5, 6, and 7 can be found in my *Adjectives and Nominalizations* (The Hague–Paris: Mouton, 1968). In writing Chapter 2, I greatly profited by the mimeographed first version of Dr. Beverly Robbins' work, *The Transformational Status of the Definite Article in English* (The Hague–Paris: Mouton, in preparation). Zellig S. Harris' recently published "Transformational Theory" (*Language* 41 [1965], 363–401) provides a short but comprehensive summary of the particular version of transformational grammar used in these works.

There are three men without whose influence these essays could not have been written: Paul Ziff, who taught me philosophy; Zellig S. Harris, who taught me linguistics; and J. L. Austin, who made me see the connection of the two. In addition I want to acknowledge the help of the members of the National Science Foundation Project in Linguistic Transformations, Department of Linguistics, University of Pennsylvania—especially that of Henry Hiż. Finally, I owe to Max Black the stimulation and encouragement to put this book together.

PREFACE

I gratefully acknowledge the permission of the editors of *The Philosophical Review* to reprint the articles "Verbs and Times" and "The Grammar of Goodness"; of the editor of *Mind* to reprint the article "Each and Every, Any and All"; and of Professor R. J. Butler, editor of the volume *Analytical Philosophy* (Oxford: Blackwell, 1962), to reprint, in part, the paper "Effects, Results and Consequences." I also wish to thank Professors Max Black and Terence M. Penelhum for a number of stylistic suggestions.

ZENO VENDLER

University of Calgary
December 1966

Contents

Linguistics *in* Philosophy

Aus dem gemeinen Erkenntnisse die Begriffe heraussuchen, welche gar keine besondere Erfahrung zum Grunde liegen haben und gleichwohl in aller Erfahrungserkenntniss vorkommen, von der sie gleichsam die blosse Form der Verknüpfung ausmachen, setzte kein grösseres Nachdenken oder mehr Einsicht voraus, als aus einer Sprache Regeln des wirklichen Gebrauchs der Wörter überhaupt heraussuchen und so Elemente zu einer Grammatik zusammentragen (in der That sind beide Untersuchungen einander auch sehr nahe verwandt), ohne doch eben Grund angeben zu können, warum eine jede Sprache gerade diese und keine andere formale Beschaffenheit habe, noch weniger aber, dass gerade so viel, nicht mehr noch weniger, solcher formalen Bestimmungen derselben überhaupt angetroffen werden können.

KANT, *Prolegomena*

[1]

Linguistics and the *A Priori*

1.1. The best way to show that a thing can be done is to do it: according to the old maxim, *valet illatio ab esse ad posse*. In the following pages I shall draw several philosophical conclusions on the basis of various applications of structural linguistics. Yet, as appears from a good number of oral and written exchanges, there is a strong current of opinion challenging the possibility of such a move. Moreover, and this gives me pause, the opposing voices are not restricted to philosophers who are skeptical toward any kind of linguistic approach, nor even to those who regard appeals to ordinary language with suspicion. Indeed, the new wave of attack has been launched by authors belonging to or influenced by the Oxford School and by followers of the later Wittgenstein—by philosophers, in other words, who are very much concerned with ordinary language. Gilbert Ryle, for instance, in his "Ordinary Language" and more explicitly in "Use, Usage and Meaning," seems to imply that the results of linguistic science have no utility on the level of philosophical analysis.[1] And Stanley Cavell, in his "Must We Mean What We Say?" and "The Availability of Wittgenstein's Later Philosophy," makes the same claim even more forcefully than Ryle, and from a strictly Wittgensteinian point of view.[2] This reluctance of philosophers of ordinary language to use the science of that language as a tool in their labors needs to be understood, explained, and if possible overcome, before I, and other people working along similar lines, can be sure of not being deluded in our efforts.

1.2. This need, at least to my mind, has not been sufficiently answered in the capable papers by William P. Alston [3] and by Jerry A. Fodor and J. J. Katz.[4] In the first place I do not think that these authors sufficiently appreciate the difficulties arising out of the claim that philosophical statements are *a priori*. This is what Fodor and Katz write:

That Cavell's position blocks an adequate understanding of ordinary language philosophy follows from the fact that the Oxford philosopher, when he discusses the use of words, *is* pursuing an empirical investigation, and *is not* uncovering truths of transcendental logic. . . . What has until now distinguished the Oxford philosopher from the linguist is primarily a differ-

---

[1] G. Ryle, "Ordinary Language," *Philosophical Review*, LXII (1953), 167–186; "Use, Usage and Meaning," *Proceedings of the Aristotelian Society*, supp. vol. XXV (1961), pp. 223–230.

[2] S. Cavell, "Must We Mean What We Say?" *Inquiry*, I (1958), 172–212; "The Availability of Wittgenstein's Later Philosophy," *Philosophical Review*, LXXI (1962), 67–93.

[3] W. P. Alston, "Philosophical Analysis and Structural Linguistics," *Journal of Philosophy*, LIX (1962), 709–720.

[4] J. A. Fodor and J. J. Katz, "What is Wrong with the Philosophy of Language?" *Inquiry*, V (1962), 197–237; "The Availability of What We Say," *Philosophical Review*, LXXII (1963), 57–71.

ence of focus. The linguist has traditionally been concerned with problems of phonology, phonemics, morphology, and syntax, while the Oxford philosopher has devoted himself almost exclusively to problems about meaning. What has distinguished some Oxford philosophers is their ingenuity at discovering recondite facts about how English speakers use their language. But methods of confirmation and disconfirmation distinguish neither the philosopher from the linguist nor the philosopher himself.[5]

What emerges from this text is the idea that the Oxford philosopher is nothing but an ingenious amateur linguist exploring certain hitherto neglected features of our language. No doubt, philosophers of ordinary language may, and very often do, give linguistic facts in support of their conclusions. But these conclusions do not fall within the domain of linguistic science: they are philosophical conclusions and the authors who draw them are doing philosophy and not linguistics.

If the assumption of Fodor and Katz were right, then scientific linguistics would tend to replace linguistic philosophy. Alston, though more cautious than Fodor and Katz, foresees exactly such a development:

Even though the analysis of language in purely formal terms does not itself give the philosopher the result he needs for his purposes, it might well separate out classes that the philosopher would find it profitable to examine in his own way. That is, the class distinctions the linguist discovers by formal procedures might parallel important conceptual distinctions, and the presentation of such formal results might provide the philosopher with hints for such distinctions. . . . And, of course, if and when semantics is developed and integrated into structural linguistics along with grammar, the differences between the two

[5] "The Availability of What We Say," p. 71.

[3]

sorts of enquiry in methods and status of conclusions, though not in ultimate aim, may well be reduced to the vanishing point.[6]

Here again I would like to deny that the "methods and status of conclusions" of linguistics and philosophy can ever be the same. True, the philosopher may use linguistic data, found by himself or borrowed from the expert, but he will go beyond these in establishing conclusions of an entirely different logical status.

1.3.   There are two other suggestions touching upon the relation of linguistics and philosophy put forward by Fodor and Katz. In their article "What is Wrong with the Philosophy of Language?" they propose that "the philosophy of language should be considered as nothing other than the philosophy of linguistics: a discipline analogous in every respect to the philosophy of psychology, the philosophy of mathematics, the philosophy of physics, etc."[7] This would amount to a mere terminological suggestion (though even so a misleading one) were it not for the fact that the authors keep regarding positivists like Carnap and ordinary language philosophers like Ryle as philosophers of language who went about their task in a wrong way. Consequently, what is wrong with their philosophy is that they did not do something different from what they were actually doing. Fortunately, at least Katz recognizes the error of this position in a later work.[8] He proposes instead the view that the philosophy of language is an investigation of conceptual knowledge based upon the general theory of language, which is "the theory in descriptive linguistics that repre-

[6] *Ibid.*, pp. 719–720.
[7] "What Is Wrong with the Philosophy of Language," p. 221.
[8] J. J. Katz, *The Philosophy of Language*, p. 4, n. 2.

[4]

sents the facts about linguistic structure common to all natural languages." [9] Although I am more sympathetic toward
this view, it still appears to me too narrow, since, as I believe and hope to show, even the linguistic data giving the
structure of a particular natural language are a fruitful
source of genuine philosophical insight.

1.4. Katz's hesitation about the nature of the philosophy
of language is indicative of a serious conceptual confusion
that pervades most recent studies, anthologies, and text-
books in the field. I think I am justified in pausing for a
moment to mark off some of the distinct ingredients from
the multifarious content of the catch-all phrase, philosophy
of language. First of all, there is indeed, or at least there
should be, *a philosophy of linguistics*. This comprises philosophical reflections on such linguistic universals as meaning, synonymy, paraphrase, syntax, and translation, and a
study of the logical status and verification of linguistic
theories. Accordingly, the philosophy of linguistics is one
of the special branches of the philosophy of science, like
the philosophy of physics, of psychology, and so on. This
discipline would be quite distinct from another, which I
would prefer to call *linguistic philosophy*. This would com-
prise conceptual investigations of any kind based upon the
structure and functioning of natural or artificial languages.
Examples of this kind of study could range from Aristotle's
reflections on being to Russell's theory of descriptions and
Ryle's work on mental concepts. The catch-all phrase,
philosophy of language, could be retained to label the re-
mainder of the original domain, still containing more or less
philosophical works on the nature of language, its relation
to reality, and so forth. Whorf's *Language, Thought and*

[9] *Ibid.*, p. 8.

Reality,[10] and perhaps Wittgenstein's *Tractatus*,[11] would remain in this category. It is possible that the science of linguistics and the philosophy of linguistics may jointly come to replace the philosophy of language—in much the same way as the physical sciences, together with the philosophy of science, have replaced, to a large extent, the cosmological speculations of the past. Linguistic philosophy, on the other hand, can only gain by an increased understanding of how language works, but will never be absorbed by linguistics plus its philosophy. In the light of these distinctions, it will be obvious that the main part of this book falls squarely into the realm of linguistic philosophy.

1.5. In the passage quoted above, Alston seems to imply that the philosophically interesting results of linguistics have been hitherto confined to grammar. This, I think, is a fair statement of the *de facto* situation. For, although the first attempts toward the formulation of a semantic theory have been made by Paul Ziff [12] and by Fodor and Katz,[13] we are not even at the beginning of the enormous empirical work that could produce semantic data in a scientific sense.

The fact that linguistic science cannot, thus far, give us semantic data, and that consequently we still have to rely on intuition in semantic matters, is certainly part of the reason why people like Ryle and Cavell do not see much hope in linguistics for philosophy. For, after all, they are primarily concerned with semantic problems: questions about what certain words mean. Take the standard illustra-

[10] B. L. Whorf, *Language, Thought and Reality*.

[11] L. Wittgenstein, *Tractatus Logico-Philosophicus*.

[12] P. Ziff, *Semantic Analysis*.

[13] J. A. Fodor and J. J. Katz, "The Structure of Semantic Theory," in Fodor and Katz (eds.), *The Structure of Language*, pp. 473–518.

[6]

tion used in the Cavell versus Fodor and Katz controversy about the relevance of linguistics to philosophy.[14] Ryle had claimed that the philosophically important word *voluntarily* is used only in connection with actions that seem to have been someone's fault. Austin denied this by pointing out that one can make a gift voluntarily. Then Cavell strikes a middle course by suggesting that at least there must be "something fishy" about the performance thus characterized. Finally Fodor and Katz reject this, referring to the possibility of joining the army voluntarily, in which case nothing fishy need be involved. Now who is right? More important, what can, or rather what does, linguistic science offer us here? The answer is simple: beyond a hope, nothing. Even the best dictionaries are notoriously wrong about philosophically important words. No wonder, then, that Ryle and Cavell remain skeptical.

What they overlook, however, is that another part of linguistics, namely syntax, is in better shape. Owing to some advances made in the last decade or so, which really amount to a break-through, we now have a fairly elaborate and quite powerful grammar of the English language, which, even if not complete and unified, is very serviceable in handling individual problems.[15] If, therefore, one raises the question whether linguistics is relevant to philosophy, one cannot, in fairness, answer it by showing that an embryonic branch of linguistics, semantics, fails in this respect. But, then, does syntax have anything to offer the philosopher who is interested in conceptual problems? Yes, it does. This

[14] Discussion and references in "The Availability of What We Say."

[15] N. Chomsky, *Syntactic Structures;* J. A. Fodor and J. J. Katz (eds.), *The Structure of Language;* Z. S. Harris, "Transformational Theory," *Language* 41 (1965), 363–401.

is so because the meaning of a word is to a large extent—but, of course, by no means entirely—a function of its syntactic constraints. To mention the most obvious example: that a word is a noun, verb, adjective, or adverb is nothing but a piece of syntactic information indicating the role of the word in sentence structures. And, surely, knowing its grammatical category is the first step in understanding the meaning of the word. But fortunately, as we shall see, syntax does not stop here: there are a great many other things it can tell us pertinent to the meaning of words. Some of these things, moreover, bear upon lively issues of contemporary philosophy, issues about which even the most prominent linguistic philosophers have been sorely mistaken precisely because their otherwise excellent intuition was not aided by the grammatical insight obtainable by means of structural and transformational linguistics.

1.6. I am aware that a mere appeal to the practical impotence of semantics is not sufficient to explain the reluctance that some people, like Ryle and Cavell, feel toward admitting linguists to the pastures of philosophy. They also produce arguments, and persuasive ones at that, to show that the results of linguistics cannot possibly support philosophical conclusions. If these arguments are sound, then no matter how many illustrations I may produce, I still must labor under an illusion—for just as it is true that *contra factum non valet argumentum*, it is also true that *contra argumentum bonum non existit factum*. I shall now survey these arguments. In doing so I shall not restrict myself to the reasons offered by Ryle and Cavell, but shall broaden and strengthen them in such a way as to express some qualms of authors who also oppose ordinary language philosophy in general.

[8]

The first objection is a formidable one. It may run as follows: the results of linguistics are empirical generalizations and, as such, express contingent facts. Philosophical statements, on the other hand, are not empirical generalizations and cannot be supported by such. *Ergo,* no linguistic result can amount to a philosophical assertion, nor can it support one. The first premise of this argument is taken for granted by the linguists themselves, and Fodor and Katz, following Noam Chomsky, lay great stress upon the similarity of linguistics to other empirical sciences. The hypothetico-deductive superstructure employed in modern linguistics only reinforces this analogy. The second premise, concerning the *a priori* nature of philosophy, may be debated in some quarters, but it is generally upheld by my opponents and I am willing to debate the issue on their own ground. It is interesting to note that the very words of the chief defender of the purity of philosophy are summoned to make the point clear. What philosophers are interested in, says Cavell, is the *a priori,* based upon the "categorical declaratives" of the native speaker.[16] R. M. Hare is tempted to speak of synthetic *a priori* propositions in a similar context.[17] The philosopher, to quote Wittgenstein himself, "is directed not towards phenomena, but, as one might say, towards the *'possibilities'* of phenomena." [18] His syntax is "logical" syntax, his logic, for Cavell again, is "transcendental," not merely formal or semantic.[19] And the grammar he wants to explore is "depth"-grammar: [20] "It is a knowl-

[16] "Must We Mean What We Say?" pp. 131 ff.

[17] R. M. Hare, "Are Discoveries about the Uses of Words Empirical?" *Journal of Philosophy,* LIV (1957), 741–750.

[18] L. Wittgenstein, *Philosophical Investigations,* I, 90.

[19] "Must We Mean What We Say?" pp. 181–182.

[20] J. N. Findlay, "Use, Usage and Meaning," *Proceedings of the Aristotelian Society,* supp. vol. XXXV (1961), pp. 231–242.

edge of what Wittgenstein means by grammar—the knowledge Kant calls 'transcendental.' " [21] In Ryle's terminology: "The Rules of Logical Syntax . . . belong not to a Language or Languages, but to Speech." [22] This tendency to take shelter under the mantle of Kant against the foray of linguists into the fields of philosophy is quite understandable as we evoke the spectre that caused the alarm, the phantom arising out of the work of some overzealous champions of "linguistics for philosophy." Can philosophical problems ever be solved by interviewing native informants, recording conversations, and committing a written corpus to the care of a computer? . . .

But then, is the argument valid? It is not. And the really interesting thing is not that it is invalid in spite of the premises' being true, but that people like Cavell do not realize its invalidity in spite of clearly seeing the point that makes it so. I shall soon restate that point myself.

1.7. Before doing so, however, I must mention two other arguments, which, no doubt, are connected with the first. One of these is as old as the rise of contemporary linguistic philosophy. From the very beginning, philosophers of ordinary language tried to protect themselves against the charge that no genuine philosophical problem can be handled on the basis of the peculiarities of a particular language. Quite recently, however, Tsu-Lin Mei has shown that a good many of the linguistic reasons P. F. Strawson uses to support his conclusions in "Proper Names" and *Individuals* fail in Chinese,[23] and I myself have been reminded by H. H.

[21] "The Availability of Wittgenstein's Later Philosophy," p. 86.
[22] "Use, Usage and Meaning," p. 230.
[23] Tsu-Lin Mei, "Subject and Predicate, a Grammatical Preliminary," *Philosophical Review*, LXX (1961), 153–175.

Dubs that some of the arguments in my paper "Verbs and Times" could not be conducted in Chinese.[24] Chinese being somewhat inaccessible to most of us, I select a more familiar example to illustrate the point. Since Ryle's discussion in *The Concept of Mind*, some obviously philosophical conclusions have been drawn from the fact that certain crucial verbs like *know*, *believe*, or *love*, unlike, say, *run*, *study*, or *think*, have no continuous tenses. While I can say that I am studying geometry, I cannot say that I am knowing geometry. For this and similar reasons, philosophers have concluded that while studying and the like are actions or processes, knowing and the like are states or dispositions. The trouble, however, is that this distinction cannot be made in German or French—or, indeed, in most of the Indogermanic languages. And how should one know that other arguments of this kind will hold in languages other than English? What shall we say then? That, for instance, knowing is not a process in English? But what sort of a philosophical thesis is this? Or shall we do comparative linguistics before making a philosophical claim? What we definitely should not do is to say what Ryle does in "Ordinary Language": "Hume's question was not about the word 'cause'; it was about the *use* of 'cause.' It was just as much about the *use* of 'Ursache.' For the use of 'cause' is the same as the use of 'Ursache,' though 'cause' is not the same word as 'Ursache.' "[25] This is an incredible claim. How does Ryle know, without an exhaustive study of both languages, that the use of *Ursache* is the same as that of *cause*? How, moreover, can two words ever have the same use in two different languages that do not show a one-to-one correlation of

[24] H. H. Dubs, "Language and Philosophy," *Philosophical Review*, LXIV (1958), 437.
[25] "Ordinary Language," p. 171.

morphemes and syntactic structures? Anyway, insofar as Ryle's claim is understandable it is obviously false: the word *cause* is both a noun and a verb. *Ursache*, on the other hand, is never a verb. And this, I say, is quite a difference in use. As for Hume, I shall have the opportunity to show that his use of *cause* has very little to do with the normal English use of that word.[26] To him, as to Locke before him, and to most philosophers in their tradition, tables and chairs would be caused by the carpenter. Yet the sentence *This chair is caused by Jones* is very odd, to say the least. Now the plot really thickens. Is the philosopher interested in Hume's use of the word *cause?* Then he should take up a Hume concordance, if there is one. Is he interested in the way English speakers at large use the word *cause?* Then he should start the enormous empirical study that the task requires. Or does he aim at finding a common denominator of *cause, Ursache, causa,* αἰτία or ἀρχή (which one?) and so on, which would commit him to the still more formidable task of a comparative linguistic study. But I have to remind the reader that our philosopher is unwilling to do any of these empirical studies. His results are *a priori;* his syntax is logical syntax; his grammar is depth-grammar.

1.8.   This leads us to the third argument, involving the "categorical declaratives" of Cavell's "native speaker." [27] Cavell presents the argument in the framework and in the phraseology of the later Wittgenstein. The result is a somewhat "mystical" doctrine about what philosophical inquiry ought to be. If we pare away the trimmings of mysticism, we are left with something like the following. The philos-

[26] See Chapter 6.
[27] "Must We Mean What We Say?" and "The Availability of Wittgenstein's Later Philosophy."

opher is a native speaker with a mastery of his language, arguing with himself or with other native speakers. Having a mastery of the language means that the speaker does not need evidence for statements (categorical declaratives) of the following sort: "In those circumstances *we* would say . . ." or "Such a thing *we* would call. . . ." "He is asking something which can be answered by remembering what is said and meant, or by trying out his own response to an imagined situation." [28] Since the language is *our* language, we will find out things about ourselves, or, rather, we will remind ourselves of certain things about the way *we* think, things we overlooked or got confused. Cavell quotes Wittgenstein: "It is of the essence of our investigation that we do not seek to learn anything *new* by it. We want to *understand* something that is already in plain view." [29] But what if *I* discover that *you* would talk differently? Well, then *this* is the discovery; the insight making me realize that "one human being can be a complete enigma to another," that "We do not *understand* the people," that "Wir können uns nicht in Sie finden." [30] The result of philosophy is self-knowledge: knowledge of *ourselves*, and knowledge of *my*self, who may be different from *others*. Then what can all the results of linguistics tell me about the way I think? How can it help me to overcome the confusions in my thinking? Whatever one may think of the method of the *Investigations*, Cavell's interpretation seems to be a faithful and instructive rendering of Wittgenstein's thought. I would be the last person to underrate Wittgenstein's method. I do not think, however, that it makes lin-

[28] "The Availability of Wittgenstein's Later Philosophy," p. 86.

[29] *Philosophical Investigations*, I, 89.

[30] *Ibid.*, II, p. 223. The given translation, "We cannot find our feet with them," is not literal enough.

guistic data irrelevant, provided their role in philosophical reasoning is properly understood.

1.9. The fundamental consideration on the basis of which I want to defend linguistics as a philosophical tool and to refute the three arguments just presented is not at all original. It is, in fact, a commonplace these days to compare language with games or with other, shall we say, rule-governed forms of behavior. The role of language-games is central in the *Investigations*, and analogies to chess, bridge, and even the eightsome reel abound in the literature.[31] The point of the analogy is fairly clear. The use of language, like the playing of a game, presupposes certain norms to which the speaker, or the player as such, has to adhere, but from which he can deviate at will. He can, in other words, be correct or incorrect, right or wrong, in what he does. This is quite different from other aspects of human behavior, or from the processes of nature. True, they too are governed by certain laws, but if deviations occur, these deviations remain aspects of human behavior, remain processes of nature. So that any variance with the law is not a shortcoming of nature, but a shortcoming of the law. The perihelion motion of Mercury deviated from Newton's laws, consequently these laws had to be amended and Mercury could not be blamed for violating the rule. If, however, I play chess and suddenly start moving a Pawn backward, then I am to be blamed for violating the rule and not the rule for failing to account for my move. For, after all, my move was not really a move; it is the rule that determines what counts as a move. There is no need to pursue

[31] Hare, "Are Discoveries about the Uses of Words Empirical?" In my own discussion, I am particularly indebted to M. Black, "Necessary Statements and Rules," *Philosophical Review*, LXVI (1958), 313–341.

the chess analogy any further; its application to language is quite familiar.

Yet I want to make a couple of remarks that bear upon the analogy. First, I would like to point out that chess is not a very fortunate example, inasmuch as it is a strictly codified and highly exact game. Language, on the other hand, is certainly not. Nobody knows better than professional linguists the flexibility of linguistic rules and their tolerance with respect to factors of time, region, variety of discourse, and individual style. Yet, in spite of this, language remains a rule-governed activity in the sense that the native speaker, in all his freedom, still maintains that he is speaking the language; that is to say, he will permit other speakers to use the same expressions: if something is understandable *from* him, it is understandable *to* him. In a similar way, in the playing of a game with loose rules, like war games or hide-and-seek, a participant may resort to some unexpected stratagem, but, if he does so in good faith, that is, in the spirit of innovation and not of cheating, he will accord the same freedom to his partners. Kant's idea of the moral agent legislating in acting is a paradigm of what I want to say here. One can even formulate the "categorical imperative" of all games: do whatever you would permit others to do in the same game. And for language: say whatever you would accept from other speakers of the same language. Then we see that language can remain rule-governed in the strictest sense, even with loose or changing rules. A given set of rules, like the ones we find in grammar books, may fall short in comprehension, may vary in space and time, but the regulative idea of the rule has to remain sovereign. But, and this is to anticipate, we should remind ourselves of Kant's warning that regulative ideas do not yield synthetic *a priori* propositions.

The second consideration I wish to offer concerns a

radical difference between language and games like chess, bridge, or hide-and-seek. Whereas talking about chess does not consist in making chess moves, in order to talk about language, or about anything, I must use language. Moreover, in describing what goes on in a chess game I have the option of using or not using chess terminology; in other words, my description of what happens might be entirely unaffected by the conceptual framework shaped by the rules of the game. Think of a person who is ignorant of board game. He would, to use Miss Anscombe's terminology,[32] stick to "brute facts": pieces of ivory being moved about on a checkered slab of wood. And his description, in a sense, would be complete. The conceptual framework of chess is, we might say, an optional one; we can take it or leave it. With language, the case is different. No matter how I "brutalize" the facts, even if I view talk as the production of noises in certain situations, these facts, themselves, will be framed and stated in the same "full-blown" language—will be affected, that is, by all the rules and conventions that make language what it is. Even while regarding my language as something contingent, even while envisioning alternatives such as other languages, or language-games, my "regarding" and "envisioning" will be by means of concepts crystallized out of the very matrix I wish to view "objectively." The attempt to get "out" of language, the desire for "brute facts" untainted by it, is, as Cavell puts it, a form of the "transcendental illusion." [33]

Imagine a chess player who is unable to look at the game at the level of brute facts. Yet he realizes the contingent nature of the rules. So he might say: "But it could be other-

[32] G. E. M. Anscombe, "On Brute Facts," *Analysis*, XVIII (1957–1958), 69–72.
[33] "The Availability of Wittgenstein's Later Philosophy," p. 86.

wise; Pawns might move backward too; Kings might be lost and the game carried on to final extermination," and so on. But he still speaks of Kings and Pawns and moves. And there are no such things as these without the existing rules of chess.

Users of language are like this chess player. Only the situation is radically worse: for it is conceivable that our player might learn how to escape from his mental restriction, but it is inconceivable that we can ever say anything, ask or wonder about anything, without our "bond," which, of course, is not a fetter at all, but the organ of the mind. To conclude, the conceptual framework imposed upon us by the rules of game can be cast away and we can still talk intelligently, but the conceptual framework imposed upon us by language cannot be left behind, under penalty of our being reduced to a Cratylus wagging his fingers.[34] Needless to say, the possibility of continuing the discussion in German or Chinese does not help matters. It is no "liberation" but a mere change of masters.

1.10   This last point looms large as we begin to examine certain propositions warranted by rule-governed activities. Suppose that while watching a game of chess I see two Pawns of the same color standing in the same column. Then I say: "One of them must have taken an opposing piece in a previous move." How do I know this? Is it sufficient to say that in all chess games we ever witnessed this correlation held? No, *given the rules of the game*, the relation holds *a priori;* the contrary is not something unusual or unlikely: it is inconceivable. Nor is this an analytic connection in the Kantian sense of the term: any given position on the board is perfectly comprehensible without historical data

---

[34] Aristotle, *Met.* 1010a.

(think of chess puzzles). One might never realize the connection, but once it is noticed, one sees that it cannot be otherwise. So here we have a small example of what can be called a synthetic *a priori* judgment. No matter how trivial such an example may be, the question it makes us to ask: How are such judgments possible? is anything but trivial. It is, as we remember, the *transzendentale Hauptfrage* itself. And, on the grounds of the given example, we can suggest an answer. The rules of chess invest certain natural objects and processes with a new character and as a result certain natural relationships of these entities necessarily acquire a new value. Thus, seen through the conceptual framework constituted by the rules of the game, two contingent historical states of affairs appear to be necessarily connected. Moreover, obviously almost any "game," or, in a larger context, almost any rule-governed activity, will be the source of such propositions. And this domain may range so far as to include mathematics or the rules governing the synthesis of the manifold of experience. Remember that to Kant the understanding is "the faculty of rules." [35]

Now we see the importance of the point previously made. While it is up to us whether or not we want to play chess, and a matter of free choice whether or not we talk in chess terms, we cannot discard the conventions of language at will and still continue to ask questions and raise problems, philosophical or otherwise. Mute philosophers cannot exist. If so, then the *a priori* truths that this "game" yields will not be trivial ones, but will be the supreme and unavoidable laws of all discourse and of all conceptual thought—laws, in other words, that the philosopher is required to discover and formulate. The word "discovery" should not frighten us here: this is not a discovery of something new; it is the

[35] *Critique of Pure Reason* A 126 (N. Kemp Smith trans., p. 147).

realization of something we "knew," in a sense, all along, but never had the opportunity or the need to reflect upon. Is the chess connection mentioned above something new to a chess-player? Most likely not. Or we might get an answer like "I never thought of it, but I should have known it had anybody ever asked me." [In a similar way, the philosophical "discovery," for instance, that one cannot know that p without p being the case, is not a new fact we have to assimilate, but the realization of a connection we knew all along in using the verb correctly. And yet, as the history of philosophy shows, we need to be reminded of it lest we go astray.

Unfortunately, not all *a priori* truths arising out of chess, or out of language, are so easy to discern. Can you checkmate a lone King with a Knight and Bishop alone? You can, and this is an *a priori* truth. Yet it takes an expert to show you why. But then you will see it for yourself, much the same way as you see the truth of a theorem of geometry that has been just proved for you. Chess, as I said, is a strictly codified and, compared with language, a relatively simple game. It stands to reason, therefore, that certain truths that arise out of the very structure of language may remain hidden to the native speaker, not only because of the remoteness of their connection with the linguistic rules, but simply because some of these rules themselves remained unnoticed by the speaker. The philosopher, therefore, who is interested in connections of this nature, should welcome any help that the linguist, the professional codifier of language, can offer him.

1.11.   But the linguist is an empirical scientist, and his results are contingent statements, while the philosopher is interested in *a priori* truths. We are back to the first objec-

tion I mentioned above. Now, however, we can deal with
it.

Suppose the game of chess has not yet been codified;
people, as some actually do, learn to play by watching
games. Imagine, then, that a devoted observer wants to save
others the labor by setting down the rules of the game.
After watching a good number of games he says: "So the
game is played this way," and then he gives the rules. This,
no doubt, is an empirical study and its results are contingent
statements. For there is no necessity about *these* being the
rules. One can imagine other games played on the same
board, with the same bits of ivory. Yet, this empirical task
is a peculiar one. The observer has to be selective in what
he takes into consideration. Not all features of the players'
behavior will be relevant, nor even everything they do on
the board. For one thing, they may make illegitimate moves.
But then these will be objected to and corrected. To be
sure about what really belongs to the game, the observer
may ask the players or test them: "Can you do this?" "Is it
all right to move that piece this way?" and so forth. In
other words he will appeal not only to what they do, but
also to what they know about the game. Accordingly, his
results will not be mere empirical generalizations about
what certain people do in certain circumstances, but they
will codify what chess players regard as permissible moves
in the game. A set of rules may be said to *describe* a game
but only inasmuch as it *prescribes* how the game should be
played. Rules are prescriptive descriptions.

Some of the rules are constitutive ones. For instance,
Pawns will be defined by giving their original positions
and their possibilities of movement. Pieces that conform to
these specifications are Pawns in the game, no matter what
they look like. That these are the rules determining the

role of the piece called "Pawn" is, I repeat, a contingent fact. But suppose that our codifier then goes on to assert that consequently no two Pawns of the same color can be found in the same column without one's having had captured an opposite piece. This is no longer a contingent statement but a necessary truth, since the terminology of the assertion ("Pawn," "opposite piece," etc.) is chess terminology, understandable only in the context of the game—that is, within the conceptual framework created by the constitutive rules. And, in this framework, the proposition in question is a necessary truth. Adding the hypothetical, "in the game of chess," would be redundant, unless one had an alternative game in mind with the same terms but different interpretations. Barring this possibility, the statement is categorically true. Accordingly, there is a radical difference between the empirical task of finding the rules constitutive of the conceptual framework, and the investigation into the *a priori* correlations that obtain within that framework. I shall call the statements resulting from the former task *external* statements, and those issuing from the latter *internal* statements. Then it is clear that in spite of the logical difference between these two kinds, the external statements will be highly relevant to the establishment of the internal ones. How can you see or show that such a statement is true without implicitly, or, in more involved cases, also explicitly invoking the rules? What will be irrelevant is the fact that the rules are themselves contingent, and can be arrived at empirically.

1.12. The linguist's work is very similar to that of our chess codifier. He too is doing empirical research in order to discover contingent facts about a given language. And, once more, this empirical research will be of a peculiarly selective type, since the results he aims at will be rules that discriminate between correct and incorrect performances. So he is not a mere observer: he will ask questions about what is right and wrong in order to elicit what the native speakers know about their language. His findings will not be "brute" generalizations about vocal noises made by a tribe of the species *Homo sapiens* but a set of rules, formulated by him according to the methodological requirements of simplicity, consistency, and comprehensiveness that account for acceptable utterances of a given language. To repeat the paradoxical phrase, he will end up with prescriptive descriptions.

Yet the statement of such rules will remain contingent; there is no *a priori* necessity about *these* being the semantic and syntactic rules of a language, say, English, that is, the one used by the native inhabitants of England, the United States, and so forth. After all, there are languages with very different structures. Accordingly, a statement such as "The verb-phrase *to know that p* is used in English correctly only if *p* is true" records a contingent fact. One can imagine a language-game in which that phrase would be synonymous with *to believe firmly that p*. Another example: the linguist might conclude, "In English the verb *to cause*, with a few clearly definable exceptions, cannot take genuine nouns, but only nominalized sentences for verb object." [36] This, too, will be a contingent fact, rather in the domain of syntax than in that of semantics. But then the linguist, or the philosopher, may go on and say things like "Therefore we cannot know something that is false," or "Therefore tables and chairs, horses and cows, cannot be caused, while disturbances or revolutions can." These truths are by no means contingent: here the speaker is not talking about certain

[36] See Chapter 6.

features of the English language, but is talking about knowledge and causation. He does not mention the verbs *to know* or *to cause*, he uses them. He does not give rules constituting the conceptual framework of the language, but, talking in that very framework, expresses a truth necessitated by it. Thus, while it is possible to envision different constraints on the use of the phoneme sequence *know* or *cause*, it is impossible to grasp what knowing something false or causing a horse would be like. In much the same way, while it is possible to imagine different rules governing the moves of the piece called "Bishop," it is impossible to imagine a checkmate of a lone King achieved by a King and a Bishop alone. The first half of these two sentences envision a somewhat different language or game from what we actually have, while the second half invites us to think something impossible in the language or the game we in fact do have.

In connection with the chess example, I remarked that adding "in chess" to internal statements would be redundant unless we needed it to exclude other games with the same terminology but different rules. In the language case, it would not only be redundant but outright silly to add a similar clause to internal statements and to say, for instance, "One cannot know something false in English," or "Spinsters are not married in English." The reason for this difference is easy to see. Talking about Kings, Pawns, and Bishops is not the same thing as playing chess, so there is a possibility of these names having a different meaning in some other game. In saying, however, "One cannot know something false," I am talking English, so the possibility of interpreting the phoneme sequences according to the rules of some other language does not arise. To say things like "Having a mistress was a respectable thing in Old English but not in current English" is to make a bad joke. And to say "History

[23]

is a science in German (*Wissenschaft*) but not in French (*science*)" is not even that. It is just confusion. To conclude, a statement such as "One cannot know something false" is not true in English or for English; it is absolutely and categorically true.

1.13. In view of these reflections the first two objections mentioned above seem to evaporate. A few words will be sufficient to give formal answers.

Linguistics, as I have emphasized, is an empirical science and its findings, the rules of a language, are contingent truths. Yet this is only half of the story. We have to add that a rule, as such, has a normative as well as a descriptive function: it describes the *correct* performance. It is in this normative aspect that the rule becomes a constitutive principle of the conceptual framework of a language. Now some philosophical statements are nothing but expressions of necessary connections emerging within this conceptual framework. In supporting them, if need be, we appeal to the rule as a normative principle and not as an empirical generalization. Yet the fact remains that it takes an empirical study, albeit of a special kind, to determine what these normative principles are. Thus an argument may run as follows: "One cannot know something false, because in English the verb-phrase *to know that p* is used correctly only in case *p* is true, and this might be verified by interviewing informants, or by other suitable methods." Granted that we have to shift logical gears a couple of times in the course of the argument; yet, in the light of what we said, these shifts are characteristic of any discourse involving games and other rule-governed activities. This, I think, answers the first objection, and shows that linguistic data cannot be denied philosophical interest merely on the ground that they are empirical. This, of course, does not show that the native speaker ever needs linguistic data in his philosophical reflections, which is the point of the third objection.

1.14. Before taking that up, however, I want to answer the second objection involving the diversity of languages. Here, again, the answer has already been given. Internal statements, like the ones quoted about knowledge and causality, are unconditionally true and not only with respect to a given language, although, of course, they are formulated in a given language. "But," you ask, "could I not say the same thing, if, for instance, I were talking Chinese?" My reply is: I do not understand the phrase "the same thing" in the sentence. But I can give a kinder answer too: think of the ways in which we try to understand what the Classic Greeks meant by παιδεία or what the Germans mean by *Weltanschauung*. In such a way a foreigner, with a language radically different from English, might try to understand what we mean by *to know*. And, if he is successful, then he too will see that one cannot know something erroneously, precisely because he has succeeded in reconstructing in his own language a conceptual model sufficiently similar to the linguistic environment of the English word. This is like showing in Riemannian geometry that the internal angles of a Euclidean triangle must total 180°. It is difficult but not impossible. Wittgenstein's policy shows full awareness of the situation: he did not prohibit the translation of his work, but insisted that the original text should accompany the translation. Take the key word, *game*, from the *Investigations*. It is *Spiel* in the original. And this word has a much broader application than *game*. Think of *Schauspiel* (theater play) or *Festspiel* (festival).

If we realize this, then we are less tempted to object to Wittgenstein's claim that there is no common characteristic to all games, by citing some such thing as competition. *Game* might connote competition, *Spiel* does not. *Game* seems to be the best translation, yet not good enough. So we have to make adjustments till we are able to follow what the author meant. One more illustration. In Hungarian, as in many other languages, the use of the copula is more restricted than in English, German, Latin, or Greek, so there is no close translation for the verb *to be*. Shall we conclude, then, that Hungarians cannot understand Aristotle? Not at all; they can, but it takes some effort at the beginning. Accordingly, if you like to put it that way, a statement like *One cannot know something erroneously* is true in all languages provided it is well translated. But, as we woefully see, this is a tautology. To conclude, the philosopher must realize that the only way of arriving at conclusions that are necessarily true is to explore the necessary truths embedded in some actual language or other. For, to repeat, the regulative idea of language or thought *as such* is sterile in this respect.

1.15.   This, however, does not mean that we are trapped in the conceptual network of our native language. We may, and often do, realize that a part of that network is inadequate for some reason or other. Once upon a time a family of concepts relating to witchcraft may have been embedded in the English language. People at that time may have understood what is meant by casting a spell or being possessed by the devil, and their philosophers may have enounced some necessary truths about such states. It happened, however, that the development of science gradually appropriated the domain of application of the concepts involved, and the language of witchcraft, overshadowed by a more powerful branch, slowly withered away through disuse. Examples of similar developments could be given, ranging from harmless survivors like *the rising of the sun* to the radical reappraisal of our concept of time necessitated by the theory of relativity. In this way, concepts borrowed from the latest growth of science may coexist side by side with petrified relics of past theories. We have no reason to think that the conceptual framework of a natural language has to be consistent in all details. In ordinary discourse we muddle through somehow, and the scientist operates with his carefully sharpened conceptual tools, often ignoring the rest. The philosopher, on the other hand, whose stock in trade is concepts, cannot fail to notice a variety of infelicities, confusions, and paradoxes. No wonder, then, that he will be inclined to suggest amendments and restrictions, or to propose artificial substitutes. He is perfectly entitled to do so, provided he realizes that in making his suggestions and proposals he is still speaking a natural language, so that the very sense and relevance of what he offers depends upon the understanding of that language as it is. He who wants to rebuild the ship has to know more about it than one who merely sails it.

1.16.   During the last few years a fascinating doctrine has been developed by Chomsky and his associates.[37] They claim that humans are born with an innate device of language acquisition, which predisposes a child to the rapid learning of any natural language, inasmuch as all such lan-

---

[37] See Chomsky's symposium paper read at the Sixty-First Annual Meeting of the Eastern Division of the American Philosophical Association, Boston, Dec. 29, 1964; also J. J. Katz, *The Philosophy of Language*, pp. 240–282.

guages exhibit the same basic features. In addition to the psychological evidence, they can appeal to the fact, usually taken for granted but really surprising, that all natural languages are intertranslatable with far less difficulty than one would expect. Again, all natural languages are subject to the linguist's study, that is to say, are describable in terms of the same linguistic universals. As we mentioned above, the linguist engages in an empirical investigation of a very special sort: he wants to find out the rules of a *language*. He knows what to expect, and his expectations do not fail: he finds phonemes and morphemes, sentences, constituent structures, and transformational relations. Of course, all these facts could perhaps be explained by assuming a common origin of all languages. However this may be, it seems to be true that all human languages share some basic features. The important question, for our present purposes, is the following: do we have to restrict the philosophically relevant aspects of a language to those shared by all languages, as Katz, for instance, suggests? In view of what I said before, I see no necessity to do so. Philosophical statements mirroring some idiosyncratic aspect of a particular language are no less true than the ones corresponding to some common feature. The difference is that assertions of the former kind will be more difficult to translate than assertions of the latter kind. We can nourish the hope that philosophical statements of importance will belong to the second type. Indeed, even the finer points made by the Oxford philosophers can be translated, without much difficulty, into other languages.[38]

[38] Concerning the points made in these two paragraphs, I have been helped by discussions with Professors S. Morgenbesser and J. J. Katz.

1.17. I return finally to the third objection and face Cavell's "native speaker." Sure enough, such a person does not ordinarily need any evidence, from the linguist or from anybody else, in order to be able to talk correctly. Normally he knows, without semantic or syntactic data, what he should call a certain thing or what he would say in certain circumstances. Moreover, the native speaker is quite capable of realizing some philosophically interesting features of his language. Indeed, as far as I know, it was philosophers, and not linguists, who first pointed out the restriction governing the use of *to know* mentioned above. And, admittedly, the work of people like Austin or Ryle makes profitable reading for linguists as well. Yet, unfortunately, the "game" of language is a very involved one, and its system of rules is more complex than we think. And the philosophical pay dirt is by no means confined to the surface. With due respect to Wittgenstein, many features of our language are apt to remain hidden from us, and some of these are no less important philosophically than the ones we can locate merely by recalling what we would or would not say given such and such. We must not forget, of course, that Wittgenstein and his followers were primarily concerned with semantic problems, and, as I mentioned at the beginning, in purely semantic matters the linguist has practically no advantage over the educated layman with a good sense for words. I have yet to meet a linguist who could match Austin in discerning fine shades of meaning. It is in the domain of syntax, of the structure of language, that the difference begins to show. A competent speaker may be as well equipped as any linguist to discriminate, for instance, between *unintentionally* and *unwittingly*, because the grammar of these words is roughly the same; if, on the other hand, the difference is also a function of grammar, then the linguist will have a definite advantage over the uninstructed speaker.

The crucial differences in meaning between words like *cause* and *make, effect* and *result, fact* and *event, good* and *yellow,* are given by syntax. In many of these cases, moreover, we have to operate on a quite sophisticated level of syntax, including transformational grammar, to account for the differences. True, the philosopher might find some indications in simply reflecting upon "what can be said" and "what cannot be said," but, as appears from concrete examples, this method can be as misleading as helpful. Only in the light of a grammatical theory will the pieces fall into a coherent pattern. In a word, the facts of language do not always lie open to plain view; sometimes they are quite hidden from us. And the philosopher, native speaker though he be, needs all the help he can get to obtain the clarity and insight into the working of the language that he needs in order to arrive at his philosophical conclusions.[39]

Locke, Hume, and their successors were native speakers of English, yet they never realized that persons or objects cannot be caused, while events, processes, and states of affairs can be, obviously because they did not notice the fact that the verb object of *to cause* normally has to be a nominalized sentence. So explosions, revolutions, and the rising of the temperature can be caused, but people, horses, or chairs cannot. "But," you object, "fires or hurricanes can, and these words are not nominalized sentences." True, but then the linguist will show you that these words belong to a small class of nouns that behave *as if* they were nominalized sentences; they can, for instance, take verbs like *occur,*

[39] In the following paragraphs I anticipate some of the conclusions to be reached in Chapters 5, 6, and 7.

last, take place, and adjectives like *sudden, gradual, prolonged*—which is not true of ordinary nouns like *man, horse,* and *rock.* These linguistic facts, then, will enable the philosopher to arrive at a more satisfactory view of causation.

If you say that the empiricists were not really interested in the concepts of ordinary language, then I mention G. E. Moore, who certainly was. Yet he compares *good* with *yellow,* says that they both denote simple and unanalysable qualities, obviously overlooking the enormous differences between them. The temptation to assimilate *good* to *yellow,* simply because they are both adjectives, is quickly overcome as soon as we reflect upon the fact that while a person can be good *at* something, and a thing can be good *for* something, nothing or nobody can be yellow at or for anything; that while a good thief can be a bad citizen, a yellow rose cannot be a non-yellow flower, and so on. That, in other words, while *good* is essentially attributed to a thing with respect to what it does or what can be done with it, *yellow* is not.

Finally, Austin himself tends to assimilate facts to events on the basis of "what one can say"—for instance that the collapse of the Germans can be called both a fact and an event. In this case, as far as I can see, only transformational grammar can show that *the collapse of the Germans* is an ambiguous phrase that can be interpreted either in the sense of an imperfectly, or in the sense of a perfectly nominalized sentence. What I mean is this. The phrase *the collapse of the Germans* may be taken to mean *that the Germans collapsed,* in which case the collapse of the Germans can be unlikely or surprising, can be mentioned or denied. In this sense, the collapse of the Germans is a fact. In the other sense, however, in which that collapse can be observed and followed, in which it can occur or take place, in which it can be slow, fast, or gradual, it is not a fact but an event. Indeed, the same sequence of words may identify both a fact and an event; but from this it does not follow that some facts are events, if that sequence of words is structurally ambiguous. Yet Austin, a master of English prose, misses this point because he simply follows "what can be said" in a situation in which this happens to be misleading.

Linguistics is helpful in analytic philosophy even for the native speaker. And its empirical source need not sully the transcendental purity of philosophical thought.

[2]

Singular Terms

2.1. The attempt to understand the nature of singular terms has been one of the permanent preoccupations of analytic philosophy, and the theory of descriptions is often mentioned as perhaps the most obvious triumph of that philosophy. As we read the many pages that Russell, Quine, Geach, Strawson, and others have devoted to this topic, and as we follow them in tracing the problems it raises, we cannot but agree with this concern. Perhaps the most important use of language is the stating of facts, and in order to understand this role one has to know how proper names function and what constitutes a definite description, one has to be clear about what we do when we refer to something, in particular whether in doing so we assert or only presuppose the existence of a thing, and, finally, one has to know what kind of existence is involved in the various situations.

As I have just implied, the collective effort of the philosophers in this case has been successful. In spite of some disagreements the results fundamentally converge and give us a fairly illuminating picture of the linguistic make-up and logical status of singular terms. This is a surprising fact. My expression of surprise, however, is intended as a tribute rather than an insult: I am amazed at how much these authors have got out of the precious little at their disposal. A few and often incorrect linguistic data obscured by an archaic grammar were more often than not all they had to start with. Yet their conclusions, as we shall see, anticipate in substance the findings of the advanced grammatical theory of today. Of course, they had their intuitions and the apparatus of formal logic. But, as the following chapters will show, the former often mislead and the latter tends to oversimplify. In this case the combination produced happy results, many of which will be confirmed in this chapter on the basis of strictly linguistic considerations. Thus, by a fortunate coincidence, I can start the specific part of this work with agreement rather than dissent; in view of what is to follow, a welcome *captatio benevolentiae*.

2.2.   I intend to proceed in an expository rather than polemical fashion. To begin with, I shall try to indicate the importance of singular terms for logical theory; then I shall outline the linguistic features marking such terms; and finally I shall use these results to assess the validity of certain philosophical claims.

Some philosophers regard terms as purely linguistic entities—that is, as parts of sentences or logical formulae—while others consider them as elements of certain nonlinguistic entities called propositions.[1] Since my concern, at least at the beginning, is primarily linguistic, I shall use the word *term* in accordance with the first alternative, that is,

---

[1] "Quine uses the expression 'term' in application to linguistic items only, whereas I apply it to non-linguistic items" (P. F. Strawson, *Individuals*, p. 154n).

to denote a string of words of a certain type or its equivalent in logical notation. This procedure, however, is not intended to prejudice the issue. We shall be led, in fact, by the natural course of our investigations, to a view somewhat different from the first alternative.

2.3.   The word *term* belongs to the logician's and not to the linguist's vocabulary. Although the use of *term* is not quite uniform, most logicians would agree with the following approximation. The result of the logical analysis of a proposition consists of the logical form and of the terms that fit into this form. These latter have no structure of their own; they are "atomic" elements, being, as it were, the parameters in the logical equation. But this simplicity is relative: it may happen that a term left intact at a certain level of analysis will require further resolution at a more advanced level. Russell's analysis of definite descriptions and Quine's elimination of singular terms can serve as classic examples of such a move.[2] To give a simpler illustration, while in the argument

> All philistines hated Socrates
> Some Athenians were philistines
> ∴ Some Athenians hated Socrates

the expression *hated Socrates* need not be analysed, that is, may be regarded as one term for the purposes of syllogistic logic, in the equally valid argument

> All philistines hated Socrates
> Socrates was an Athenian
> ∴ Some Athenian was hated by all philistines

[2] See, for example, B. Russell, "Descriptions," Chap. xvi in *Introduction to Mathematical Philosophy,* pp. 167–180; W. V. Quine, *Methods of Logic,* pp. 220 ff.

the expression *hated Socrates* has to be split to show validity by means of the theory of quantification.

The logical forms available to simple syllogistic logic treat all terms in a uniform fashion: any term can have universal or particular "quantity" depending upon the quantifier (*all, some*), the "quality" of the proposition (affirmative or negative), and the position of the term (subject or predicate). It is in the theory of quantification that the distinction between singular and general terms becomes explicit. For one thing, the schemata themselves may provide for such a distinction. Consider the second argument given above. It can be represented as follows:

$$(x)(Px \supset Hxs)$$
$$As$$
$$\therefore (\exists x)[Ax.\ (y)(Py \supset Hyx)]$$

Notice that the argument will not work if *Socrates* is treated like the other terms (*philistine, hated, Athenian*). Such a treatment might amount to the following:

$$(x)[Px \supset (\exists y)(Sy.Hxy)]$$
$$(\exists x)(Sx.Ax)$$
$$\therefore (\exists x)[Ax.\ (y)(Py \supset Hyx)]$$

This argument, of course, is not valid. Nevertheless, as Quine stipulated, *Socrates* may be represented as a term on par with the rest, provided a uniqueness clause is added to the premises, that is

$$(x)(y)(Sx.Sy. \supset x = y)$$

Quine's proposal thus restores the homogeneity of terms characteristic of syllogistic logic: singularity or generality becomes a function of the logical form alone. Yet, in any case, whether the logician is inclined to follow Quine or not, he at least has to realize the difference between terms like *Socrates* and terms like *philistine* or *Athenian,* and must either represent the former by an individual constant or, if he prefers homogeneity and treats it as a predicate, then add the uniqueness clause. Then the question arises how to recognize terms that require such a special consideration, in a word, how to recognize singular terms. The possibility of an "ideal" language without such terms will not excuse the logician from facing this problem if he intends to use his system to interpret propositions formulated in a natural language.

The linguistic considerations relevant to the solution of this problem are by no means restricted to the morphology of the term in question; often the whole sentence, together with its transforms or even its textual and pragmatic environment must also be considered. Granted, a logician who is a fluent speaker of the language is usually able to make a decision without explicit knowledge of the relevant factors. Such an intuition, however, cannot be used to support philosophical claims about singular terms with any authority. To provide such support and to make our intuitions explicit one has to review the "natural history" of singular terms in English, to which task I shall address myself in the following sections.

2.4. It is not an accident that in giving an example of a singular term I selected a proper name, *Socrates;* proper names are traditionally regarded as paradigms of singular terms. Owing to a fortunate convention of modern English spelling, proper names, when written, wear their credentials on their sleeves. This, however, is hardly a criterion. Many adjectives, like *English,* have to be capitalized too. Moreover, while this convention might aid the reader, it certainly does not help, in the absence of a capitalization mor-

pheme, the listener or the writer. Thus we had better remind ourselves of the linguists' *dictum* that language is the
spoken language, and look for some real marks.

First we might fall back on the intuition that proper
names have no meaning (in the sense of "sense" and not of
"reference"), which is borne out by the fact that they do
not require translation into another language. *Vienna* is the
English version and not the English translation of the German name *Wien*. Accordingly, dictionaries do not list
proper names; knowledge of proper names does not belong
to the knowledge of a language. In linguistic terms this intuition amounts to the following: proper names have no
specific co-occurrence restrictions.[3] A simple example will
illustrate this.

(1) I visited Providence

is a correct sentence, but

(2) *I visited providence

is not (here I make use of the above-mentioned convention). The word *providence* has fairly strict co-occurrence
restrictions, which exclude contexts like (2). The morphologically identical name in (1), however, waives these restrictions and permits the co-occurrence with *I visited*. . . .
Of course, our knowledge that Providence is, in fact, a city
will impose other restrictions. This piece of knowledge,
however, belongs to geography and not linguistics. That is
to say, while it belongs to the understanding of the word
providence that it cannot occur in sentences like (2), it is
not the understanding of the name *Providence* that permits

---

[3] On the notion of co-occurrence see Z. S. Harris, "Co-occurrence and Transformation in Linguistic Structure," *Language* 33
(1957), 283–340.

(1), but the knowledge that it happens to be the name of a city. From a linguistic point of view, proper names have no restrictions of occurrence beyond the broad grammatical constraints governing noun phrases in general. Indeed, only some proper names show a morphological identity with significant words; and this coincidence is of a mere historical interest: *Providence*, as a name, is no more significant than *Pawtucket*. For these reasons some linguists regard all proper names as a single morpheme. The naming of cats may be a difficult matter, but it does not enrich the language.

A little reflection will show that the very incomprehensibility of the proper names that do not coincide morphologically with significant words, and the absence of specific co-occurrence restrictions with those that do, form a valuable clue in recognizing proper names in spoken discourse. But this mark applies to proper names only and casts little light in general on the nature of singular terms, most of which are not proper names. There are, however, other characteristics marking the occurrence of proper names that will lead us to the very essence of singular terms.

2.5.   Names, as I implied above, fit into noun-phrase slots. And most of them can occur there without any additional apparatus, unlike the vast majority of common nouns, which, at least in the singular, require an article or its equivalent. The sentence

> *I visited city

lacks an article, but (1) above does not. Some common nouns, too, can occur without an article. This is true of the so-called "mass" nouns and "abstract" nouns. For instance:

> I drink water.
> Love is a many-splendored thing.

Yet these nouns, too, can take the definite article, at least when accompanied by certain "adjuncts" (italicized) in the same noun phrase: [4]

> I see the water *in the glass.*
> The love *she felt for him* was great.[5]

Later on I shall elaborate on the role of adjuncts like *in the glass* and *she felt for him.* For the time being I merely express the intuition that these adjuncts, in some sense or other, restrict the application of the nouns in question; *in the glass* indicates a definite bulk of water, *she felt for him* individuates love.

This intuition gains in force as we note that such adjuncts and the definite article are repugnant to proper names, or, if we force the issue, they destroy the very nature of such names. First of all, there is something unusual about noun phrases like

> (3) the Joe in our house
> (4) the Margaret you see.

And, notice, this oddity is not due to co-occurrence restrictions:

> (5) Joe is in our house
> (6) You see Margaret

are perfectly natural sentences. The point is that while sentences like

---

[4] The technical notion, "the phrase x is an adjunct of the phrase y," roughly corresponds to the intuitive notion of one phrase "modifying" another. See Z. S. Harris, *String Analysis of Sentence Structure*, pp. 9 ff.

[5] Mass nouns can take the indefinite article only in explicit or implicit combination with "measure" nouns: *a pound of meat, a cup of coffee;* phrases like *a coffee,* are products of an obvious deletion: *a [cup of] coffee.*

I see a man
Water is in the glass
He feels hatred

yield noun phrases like

the man I see
the water in the glass
the hatred he feels

sentences like (5) and (6) only reluctantly yield phrases like (3) or (4). Nevertheless such phrases do occur and we understand them. It is clear, however, that such a context is fatal to the name as a proper name, at least for the discourse in which it occurs. The full context, explicit or implicit, will be of the following sort:

The Joe in our house is not the one you are talking about.

The Margaret you see is a guest, the Margaret I mentioned is my sister.

As the noun replacer, *one*, in the first sentence makes abundantly clear, the names here simulate the status of a count noun: there are two Joe's and two Margaret's presupposed in the discourse, and this is, of course, inconsistent with the idea of a logically proper name. *Joe* and *Margaret* are here really equivalent to something like *person called Joe* or *person called Margaret*, and because these phrases fit many individuals, they should be treated as general terms by the logician.

Certain names, moreover, can be used to function as count nouns in a less trivial sense:

Joe is not *a* Shakespeare.
Amsterdam is *the* Venice of the North.

[41]

> *These little* Napoleon*s* caused the trouble in Paraguay.

Here again we can rely upon the grammatical setting to recognize them as count nouns, albeit of a peculiar ancestry.

It is harder to deal with another case of proper names with restrictive adjunct and article. I do not want to claim that the names in sentences like

> The Providence you know is no more
> You will see a revived Boston
> He prefers the early Mozart

have ceased to be proper names. Still less would I cast doubt on the credentials of proper names that seem to require the definite article, like *the Hudson, the Bronx, the Cambrian,* and so forth. The difficulties posed by these two kinds require more advanced linguistic considerations, so I shall deal with them at a later stage.

Disregarding such peripheral exceptions, we may conclude that proper names are like mass nouns in refusing the indefinite article, but are unlike them in refusing the definite article as well. And the reason seems to be that while even mass nouns or abstract nouns can take *the* when accompanied by certain restrictive adjuncts, proper names cannot take *the* since such adjuncts themselves are incompatible with proper names. Clearly, then, the intuitive notion that a proper name, as such, uniquely refers to one and only one individual has the impossibility of restrictive adjuncts as a linguistic counterpart. To put it bluntly, what is restricted to one cannot be further restricted. A proper name, therefore, is a noun which has no specific co-occurrence restrictions and which precludes restrictive adjuncts and, consequently, articles of any kind in the same noun phrase.

2.6. This latter point receives a beautiful confirmation as we turn our attention to a small class of other nouns that are also taken to be uniquely referring. These are the pronouns, *I, you, he, she,* and *it.*[6] The impossibility of adding restrictive adjuncts and the definite article is even more marked here than in the case of proper names. Yet, once more, this is not due to co-occurrence restrictions; there is nothing wrong with sentences such as

> I am in the room
> I see you.

But they will not yield the noun phrases

> *(the) I in the room
> *(the) you I see

which they would yield were the pronouns replaced by common nouns like *a man* or *water*. There is an even more striking point. Neither these pronouns nor proper names can ordinarily take prenominal adjectives. From the sentences

> He is bald
> She is dirty

we cannot get

> *bald he
> *dirty she.

---

[6] *We, you,* and *they* are used to refer to unique *groups* of individuals. Here, as in the sequel, I restrict myself to the discussion of definite noun phrases in the singular. It is clear, however, that our findings will apply *mutatis mutandis* to definite noun phrases in the plural as well: *those houses, our dogs, the children you see,* and so forth. From a logical point of view these phrases show a greater affinity to singular than to general terms. See P. F. Strawson, "On Referring," *Mind,* LIX (1950), 343–344.

And even from

> Joe is bald
> Margaret is dirty

we need poetic licence to obtain

> bald Joe
> dirty Margaret.

True, we use "Homeric" epithets, like

> lightfooted Achilles
> tiny Alice

and, in an emotive tone, we say things like

> poor Joe

or even

> poor she
> miserable you

but such a pattern is neither common nor universally productive. These facts seem to suggest that prenominal adjectives are also restrictive adjuncts. Later on we shall be able to confirm this impression.

2.7.   "A grammar book of a language is, in part, a treatise on the different styles of introduction of terms into remarks by means of expressions of that language." [7] Adopting for a moment Strawson's terminology, we can say that proper names and singular pronouns introduce singular terms by themselves without any specific style or additional linguistic apparatus. These nouns are, in fact, allergic to the restrictive apparatus which other nouns need to introduce singular terms, or, reverting to our own way of talking, the restric-

---

[7] P. F. Strawson, *Individuals*, p. 147.

[44]

tive apparatus which other nouns need to become singular terms. In this section I shall take up the task of the grammar book and investigate in detail the natural history of singular terms formed out of common nouns. My paradigms will be count-nouns, simply because they show the full scope of the restrictive apparatus of the language.

It does not require much grammatical sophistication to detect the main categories of singular terms formed out of common nouns. They will begin with a demonstrative pronoun, possessive pronoun, or the definite article—for instance, *this table, your house, the dog.* The first two kinds may be identifying by themselves, but not the third. This can be shown in a simple example. Someone says,

> A house has burned down.

We ask,

> Which house?

The answers

> That house
> Your house

may be sufficient in a given situation. The simple answer

> The house

is not. *The* alone is not enough. We have to add an adjunct that lends identifying force—for instance:

> The house you sold yesterday.
> The house in which we lived last year.

Nevertheless, in certain contexts *the* alone seems to identify. Consider the following sequence.

> I saw a man. The man wore a hat.

[45]

Obviously, the man *I saw* wore a hat. *The,* here, indicates a deleted but recoverable restrictive adjunct based upon a previous occurrence of the same noun in an identifying context. This possibility, following upon our previous findings concerning *the,* suggests a hypothesis of fundamental importance: the definite article in front of a noun is always and infallibly the sign of a restrictive adjunct, present or recoverable, attached to the noun. The proof of this hypothesis will require a somewhat technical discussion of restrictive adjuncts. But *the,* according to Russell, is "a word of very great importance," worth investigating even in prison or dead from the waist down.[8]

2.8.　My first task, then, is to give a precise equivalent for the intuitive notion of a restrictive adjunct. I claim that all such adjuncts can be reduced to what the grammarians call the restrictive relative clause. With respect to many of the examples used thus far the reconstruction of the relative clause is a simple matter indeed. All we have to know is that the relative pronoun—*which, who, that,* and so on—can be omitted between two noun phrases, and that the relative pronoun plus the copula can be omitted between a noun phrase and a string consisting of a preposition and a noun. Thus we can complete the full relative clauses in our familiar examples:

> I see the water (which is) in the glass
> The love (which) she felt for him was great
> The man (whom) I saw wore a hat
> The house (which) you sold yesterday has burned down

and so forth. If the conditions just given are not satisfied, *wh. . .* or *wh. . . is* cannot be omitted:

[8] Russell, "Descriptions," p. 167.

[46]

The man *who* came in is my brother.
The house *which is* burning is yours.

The reduction of prenominal adjectives to relative clauses is a less simple matter. In most cases, however, the following transformation is sufficient to achieve this:

(7) AN—N wh. . . is A[9]

as in

bald man—man who is bald
dirty water—water that is dirty

and so on. Later on we shall be able to show the correctness of (7).

In order to arrive at a precise notion of a restrictive relative clause, I have to say a few words about the other class of relative clauses, which are called appositive relative clauses. Some examples:

(8) You, who are rich, can afford two cars.
(9) Mary, whom you met, is my sister.
(10) Vipers, which are poisonous, should be avoided.

Our intuition tells us that the clauses here have no restrictive effect on the noun to which they are attached. *You* and *Mary*, as we recall, cannot be further restricted, and the range of *vipers* is not restricted either, since all vipers are poisonous. Indeed, (8)–(10) easily split into the following conjunctions:

(11) *You* are rich. *You* can afford two cars.
(12) You met *Mary*. *Mary* is my sister.
(13) *Vipers* are poisonous. *Vipers* should be avoided.

[9] For a detailed discussion of this and analogous transformations see Chapter 7. *Wh* . . . stands for the appropriate relative pronoun.

[47]

Thus we see that the appositive clause is nothing but a device for joining two sentences that share a noun phrase. One occurrence of the shared noun phrase gets replaced by the appropriate *wh.* . . and the resulting phrase (after some rearrangement of the word order when necessary) gets inserted into the other sentence following the occurrence of the shared noun phrase there. It is important to realize that this move does not alter the structure of the shared noun phrase in either of the ingredient sentences: the *wh.* . . replaces that noun phrase "as is" in the enclosed sentence, and the clause gets attached to that noun phrase "as is" in the enclosing sentence.[10] It is not surprising, therefore, that the whole move leaves the truth-value of the ingredient sentences intact: (8)–(10) are true, if and only if the conjunctions in (11)–(13) are true.

This is not so with restrictive clauses. Compare (10) with

(14) Snakes which are poisonous should be avoided.

If we try to split (14) into two ingredients we get

(15) Snakes are poisonous. Snakes should be avoided.

Clearly, the conjunction in (15) is false, but (14) is true. And the reason for this fact is equally obvious. The clause *which are poisonous* is an integral part of the subject of (14); the predicate *should be avoided* is not ascribed to *snakes* but to *snakes which are poisonous*, that is, by virtue of (7), to *poisonous snakes*. It appears, therefore, that while the insertion of an appositive clause merely joins two com-

[10] The shared noun phrase need not have an identical form in the original sentences. From *I bought a house, which has two stories* we recover *I bought a house. The house (I bought) has two stories.* These two sentences are continuous with respect to the noun *house.* This notion of continuity will be explained later.

plete sentences, the insertion of a restrictive clause alters the very structure of the enclosing sentence by completing one of its noun phrases. Consequently a mere conjunction of the ingredient sentences is bound to fall short of the information content embodied in the sentence containing the restrictive clause.

There are a few more or less reliable morphological clues that may help us in distinguishing these two kinds. First, appositive clauses, but not restrictive ones, are usually separated by a pause, or in writing by a comma, from the enclosing sentence. Second, *which* or *who* may be replaced by *that* in restrictive clauses, but hardly in appositive ones:

> Snakes that are poisonous should be avoided

versus

> Vipers, which are poisonous, should be avoided.

Finally, the omission of *wh*. . . or *wh*. . . *is* mentioned above works only in restrictive clauses:

> The man you met is here

versus

> *Mary, you met, is here.

2.9. I claim that the insertion of a restrictive clause after a noun is a necessary condition of its acquiring the definite article. Therefore the definite article does not belong either to the enclosing or to the enclosed sentence prior to the formation of the clause. Consider the sentence

> (16) I know the man who killed Kennedy.

If we take *the man* to be the shared noun phrase, we get the ingredients

I know the man. The man killed Kennedy.

Here *the man* suggests some other identifying device, different from the one in (16), namely *who killed Kennedy*. In the case of a proper name this line of analysis leads to outright ungrammaticality. Consider, for example,

The Providence you know is no more.

Taking *the Providence* as the shared noun phrase we get the unacceptable

*You know the Providence. *The Providence is no more.

Thus we have to conclude that the ingredient sentences do not contain the definite article; it first enters the construction after the fusion of the two ingredients. Accordingly, (16) is to be resolved into the following two sentences:

I know a man. A man killed Kennedy.

The shared noun phrase is *a man*. By replacing its second occurrence with *who* we obtain the clause *who killed Kennedy*. This gets inserted into the first sentence yielding

I know a man who killed Kennedy.

Since the verb *kill* suggests a unique agent, the definite article replaces the indefinite one, and we get (16). If the relevant verb has no connotation of uniqueness, no such replacement need take place; for instance,

I know a man who fought in Korea.

Of course we can say, in the plural,

(17) I know the men who fought in Korea.

In this case I imply that, in some sense or other, I know all those men. If I just say

> I know men who fought in Korea

no completeness is implied; it is enough if I know some such men.

It transpires, then, that the definite article marks the speaker's intention to exhaust the range determined by the restrictive clause. If that range is already restricted to one, the speaker's hand is forced: *the* becomes obligatory; a sentence like

> God spoke to a man who begot Isaac

is odd for this reason. In this case the semantics of *beget* already decides the issue. In other cases the option remains:

> I see a tree in our garden

is as good as

> I see the tree in our garden.

This latter remark, however, would be misplaced if, in fact, more than one tree is in our garden: the speaker promises uniqueness, which, in the given situation, the clause cannot deliver.

The way of producing a singular term out of a common noun is as follows: attach a restrictive clause to the noun in the singular and prefix the definite article. It may happen that the clause is not restrictive enough; its domain, in a given speech situation, may include more than one individual. This trouble is similar to the one created by saying

> Joe is hungry

when more than one person is called Joe in the house. In either case there are several possibilities: the speaker may lack some information, may be just careless, may be intentionally misleading, or some such thing. Yet *Joe* or *the tree in our garden* remain singular terms. The fact that a tool can be misused does not alter the function of the tool. Later on I shall return to infelicities of this kind.

2.10. But this is only half the story. I mentioned above that in many cases the addition of the definite article alone seems to suffice to create a singular term out of a common noun:

(18) I see a man. The man wears a hat.

Obviously, we added, the man I see wears a hat. What happened is that the clause *whom I see* got deleted after *the man*, in view of the redundancy in the full sequence

I see a man. The man I see wears a hat.

The in (18), then, is nothing but a reminder of a deleted but recoverable restrictive clause. It is, as it were, a connecting device, which makes the discourse continuous with respect to a given noun. Indeed, if *the* is omitted, the two sentences become discontinuous:

I see a man. A man wears a hat.

Hence an important conclusion: *the* in front of a noun not actually followed by a restrictive clause is the sign of a deleted clause to be formed from a previous sentence in the same discourse containing the same noun. This rule explains the continuity in a discourse like

I have a dog and a cat. The dog has a ball to play with. Often the cat plays with the ball too.

and the felt discontinuity in a text like

I have a dog and a cat. A dog has the ball.

If our conclusions are correct, then a noun in the singular already equipped with the definite article cannot take another restrictive clause, since such a noun phrase is a singular term as much as a proper name or a singular pronoun. Compare the two sequences:

(19) I see a man. The man wears a hat.
(20) I see a man. The man you know wears a hat.

(19) is continuous. *The* is the sign of the deleted clause (*whom*) *I see*. In (20) the possibility of this clause is precluded by the presence of the actual clause (*whom*) *you know*. *The* in (20) belongs to this clause and any further restrictive clauses are excluded. Consequently there is no reason to think that the man you know is the same as the man I see. Not so with appositive clauses. The sequence

I see a man. The man, whom you know, wears a hat.

is perfectly continuous. *The man*, in the second sentence, has the deleted restrictive clause (*whom*) *I see*, plus the appositive clause *whom you know*. Now consider the following pair:

(21) I see a rose. The rose is lovely.
(22) I see a rose. The red rose is lovely.

(21) is continuous, (22) is not. This fact can be explained by assuming (7), that is, by deriving the prenominal adjective from a restrictive clause, which clause then precludes the aquisition of additional restrictive clauses. The assumption of (7), as we recall, also explains the difficulties encountered in trying to attach prenominal adjectives to proper names and personal pronouns.

2.11. The story, alas, is still not complete. Think of the ambiguity in a sentence like

(23) The man she loves must be generous.

This either means that there is a man whom she loves and who must be generous, or that any man she loves must be generous. Examples of this kind can be multiplied. In some of these the generic interpretation is the obvious one. For instance,

> Happy is the man whose heart is pure.

It would be odd to continue:

> I met him yesterday.

The natural sequel is rather:

> I met one yesterday.[11]

In other cases the individual interpretation prevails:

> The man she loved committed suicide.

Yet, with some imagination, even such a sentence can be taken in the generic sense.

How do we decide which interpretation is right in a given case? In order to arrive at an answer, imagine three discourses beginning as follows:

> (24) Mary is a demanding girl. The man she loves must be generous.
> (25) Mary loves a man. The man she loves must be generous.
> (26) Mary loves a man. The man must be generous.

In (26) there is no ambiguity: *the man* is a singular term; in (25) it is likely to be a singular term; in (24) it is likely to be a general one. Why is this so? In (26) the deleted clause must be derived from the previous sentence, since, as we recall, the point of deletion is to remove redundancy. In

---

[11] It is interesting to realize that a personal pronoun, like *he*, also can occur in a generic sense—e.g., *He who asks shall be given.*

(25) the clause is most likely a derivative of the previous sentence. If so, *the man* is a singular term. It remains possible, however, to imagine a break in the discourse between the two sentences: after stating a specific fact about her the speaker begins to talk about Mary in general terms. In (24) the reverse holds: the clause cannot be derived from a previous sentence, since there is no such sentence containing the noun, *man*. Consequently *the man* will be generic, unless a statement to the effect that Mary, in fact, loves a man is presupposed. Thus the moral of these examples emerges: a phrase of the type *the N* is a singular term if its occurrence is preceded by an actual or presupposed sentence of a certain kind in which *N* occurs, in the same discourse (the qualification, "of a certain kind," will be explained soon). Accordingly, to take an occurrence of a *the N*-phrase to be a singular term is to assume the existence of such a sentence.

2.12. Since *the* always indicates a restrictive clause and since the only reason for deleting such a clause thus far mentioned is redundancy, that is, the presence of the sentence from which the clause is generated, one might conclude that no *the N*-phrase without a clause can occur if no such sentence can be found in the previous portion of the discourse. Yet this is not so. Some clause-less *the N*-phrases can occur at the very outset of a discourse. These counterexamples fall into three categories.

The first class comprises utterances of the following type:

> The castle is burning.
> The president is ill.

In these cases the clauses (*in our town, of our country*) are omitted simply because they are superfluous in the given

[55]

situation. Such *the N*-phrases, in fact, approximate the status of proper names: they tend to identify by themselves. It is not surprising, therefore, that they are often spelled with a capital letter: *the President, the Castle.* To a small circle of speakers even more common nouns can acquire this status:

Did you feed the dog?

The second category amounts to a literary device. One can begin a novel as follows:

The boy left the house.

Such a beginning suggests familiarity: the reader is invited to put himself into the picture: he is "there," he sees the boy, he knows the house.

2.13.   The third kind is entirely different. It involves a generic *the* without an actual clause. Examples abound:

(27) The mouse is a rodent
(28) The tiger lives in the jungle
(29) The Incas did not use the wheel

and so forth. It is obvious that no clause restricting *mouse, tiger,* or *wheel* is to be resurrected here: the ranges of these nouns remain unrestricted. Shall we, then, abandon our claim that the definite article always presupposes a restrictive clause? We need not and must not. In order to see this, consider the saying:

None but the brave deserves the fair.

The obvious paraphrase is

None but the [man who is] brave deserves the [woman who is] fair.

This suggests the following deletion pattern:

the N wh . . . is A $\rightarrow$ the A

Then it is easy to see that sentences like

This book is written for the mathematician
Only the expert can give an answer

contain products of a similar pattern, to wit:

(30) the N_i wh . . . is an $N_j \rightarrow$ the N_j

Thus *the mathematician* and *the expert* come from *the [person who is a] mathematician* and *the [person who is an] expert*. And similarly, for (27)–(29) the sources are:

the [animal that is a] mouse (tiger)
the [instrument that is a] wheel.

We have seen above that a redundant clause can be omitted. In (30) a redundant noun, N_i, is omitted and *the* is transferred to N_j. N_i is redundant because it is nothing but N_j's genus, and as such easily recoverable. This suggests that nouns that are themselves too generic to fall under a superior genus are not subject to (30). This is indeed so. While

Tigers live in the jungle
The Incas did not use wheels

do have (28) and (29) as paraphrases, sentences like

Objects are in space
Monkeys do not use instruments

are not paraphraseable into

The object is in space
Monkeys do not use the instrument.[12]

---

[12] The existence or nonexistence of a higher genus may be a function of the discourse. In philosophical writing, for instance,

In these sentences the *the* N-phrases have to be singular terms, consequently we are looking for the sentences from which the identifying clauses belonging to *the object* and *the instrument* are to be derived: what object (instrument) are we talking about?

This last point may serve as an indirect proof of (30). A more direct proof is forthcoming from the following example:

> There are two kinds of large cat living in Paraguay, the jaguar and the puma.

Obviously, *the jaguar and the puma* is derived from

> the [(kind of) large cat that is a] jaguar and the [(kind of) large cat that is a] puma.

In this case, unlike some of the previous examples, neither *a jaguar and a puma* nor *jaguars and pumas* will do to replace the generic *the jaguar and the puma*. Thus the generic *the* is not a mere variant of other generic forms. It has an origin of its own. Another illustration:

> Euclid described the parabola.

The parabola here is inadequately paraphrased by *a parabola*, *parabolas* or *all parabolas*. The given solution works again:

> Euclid described the [(kind of) curve that is a] parabola.

Incidentally, although we might say

> Euclid described curves

we cannot express this by saying

---

one might find a generic sentence like *The idea is more perfect than the object*, which presupposes a common genus for ideas and objects.

[58]

Euclid described the curve.

Curve is too generic.[13]

2.14. The possibility of transferring *the* from an earlier noun, exemplified in (30), indicates a solution for noun phrases containing a proper name with the definite article. *The Hudson, the early Mozart, the Providence you know* are most likely derived from

the [river called] Hudson
the early [period/works of] Mozart
the [aspect/appearance of] Providence you know.

Indeed, it can be shown that the clause *you know*, for instance, does not belong to *Providence* directly. For if it did, the following sequence would be acceptable:

You know Providence.* The Providence is no more.

on the analogy of, say,

You had a house. The house is no more.

In this case the first sentence yields the clause *which you had*, which clause justifies *the* before *house* in the second sentence. In the previous example, however, the first sentence refuses to yield the clause *which you know*, precisely because *Providence* is a proper name. Thus *Providence* in the second sentence has no clause to justify *the*. Consequently *the Providence you know* does not come directly from

You know Providence.

2.15. Owing to the inductive nature of our investigations up to this point, our conclusions concerning the formation

---

[13] As man is an exceptional animal, *man* is an exceptional noun. It has a generic sense in the singular without any article: *Man, but not the ape, uses instruments.*

of singular terms out of common nouns had to be presented in a provisional manner leaving room, as it were, for the variety of facts still to be accounted for. Now, in retrospect, we are able to give a more coherent picture, at least in its main lines, for many details of this very complex affair must be left to further studies. The basic rules seem to be the following:

(a) The definite article is a function of a restrictive clause attached to the noun.

(b) This article indicates that the scope of the so restricted noun is to be taken exhaustively, extending to any and all objects falling under it.

(c) If the restriction is to one individual the definite article is obligatory and marks a singular term. Otherwise the term is general and the definite article remains optional.

(d) The clause is restrictive to one individual if and only if it is derived from a sentence either actually occurring in the previous part of the same discourse, or presupposed by the same discourse, and in which sentence N has an identifying occurrence. This last notion remains to be explained.

(e) Redundant clauses can be omitted.

(f) A clause is redundant if it is derived from a sentence actually occurring in the previous part of the discourse, or if the information content of a sentence in which N has an identifying occurrence is generally known to the participants of the discourse.

(g) Redundant genus nouns can be omitted according to (30).

2.16.　These rules give us the following recognition-procedure with respect to any *the* N-phrase, where N is a common noun.

(i) If the phrase is followed by a clause look for the mother sentence of the clause.

(ii) If it is found, and if it identifies N, the phrase is a singular term. If it fails to identify, the phrase is a general term.

(iii) If no mother sentence can be found, ask whether the circumstances of the discourse warrant the assumption of an identifying sentence corresponding to the clause.

(iv) If the answer is in the affirmative, we have a singular term, otherwise a general one.

(v) If the phrase is not followed by a clause, look for a previous sentence in which N occurs without the definite article.

(vi) If there is such an occurrence the deleted clause after the phrase is to be recovered from that sentence.

(vii) If that occurrence is identifying we have a singular term, otherwise a general one.

(viii) If there is no such occurrence, ask whether the circumstances of the discourse warrant the assumption of a sentence that would identify N to the participants of the discourse.

(ix) If the answer is in the affirmative we have a singular term and the clause is to be recovered from that sentence.

(x) If the answer is in the negative *the N* is a general term with a missing genus to be recovered following (30).

In order to have an example illustrating the various possibilities for a singular term of the *the N* type, consider the following. My friend returns from a hunt and begins:

> Imagine, I shot a bear and an elk. The bear I shot nearly got away, but the elk dropped dead on the spot. Incidentally, the gun worked beautifully, but the map you gave me was all wrong.

The bear I shot is a singular term by (ii). *The elk* is singular by (vii) with the clause *I shot* according to (vi). *The gun* is singular by (ix) with a clause something like *I had with me; the map you gave me* is singular by (iv).

The appeal to the circumstances of the discourse found in (iii) and (viii) is admittedly a cover for an almost inexhaustible variety of relevant considerations. Some of these are linguistic, others pragmatic. Tensed verbs suggest singular terms, modal contexts general ones. But think of the man Mary loves, who must be generous, and of the dinosaur, which roamed over Jurassic plains. In practice it may be impossible to arrive at a verdict in many situations. You may have only one cat, yet your wife's remark

The cat is a clever beast

may remain ambiguous. What is important to us is rather the universal presupposition of all singular terms of the *the N* type: the actual or implied existence of an identifying sentence. This notion still remains to be explained.

2.17. Once more I shall proceed in an inductive manner. First I shall enumerate the main types of identifying sentence and then try to find some common characteristics.

First of all, a sentence identifies *N* if it connects *N* with a definite noun phrase in a noncopulative and nonmodal fashion. The class of definite noun phrases comprises all singular terms and their plural equivalents like *we, you, they, these boys, my daughters, the dogs,* and so forth. Consequently the following sentences are identifying ones:

(31) I see a house. The house . . .
(32) They dug a hole. The hole . . .
(33) The dogs found a bone. The bone . . .

The order of the noun phrases does not matter:

(34) A snake bit me. The snake . . .

PN adjuncts also connect both ways:

> (35) They dug a hole with a stick. The stick . . .
> (36) A boy had dinner with me. The boy . . .

and so forth.

It follows that definite nouns of the *the* N-type can form a chain of identification. For instance:

> I see a man. The man wears a hat. The hat has a feather on it. The feather is green.

But, of course, all chains must begin somewhere. This means that at the beginning of most discourses containing definite nouns, there must occur a "basic" definite noun: a personal pronoun, a proper name, or a noun phrase beginning with a demonstrative or possessive pronoun. By these terms, as it were, the whole discourse is anchored in the world of individuals.

Copulative verbs like *be* and *become* do not connect. The following sequences remain discontinuous:

> (37) He is a teacher. The teacher is lazy.
> (38) Joe became a salesman. The salesman is well paid.

We know, of course, that these two verbs are peculiar in other respects too. Their verb object does not take the accusative and the sentences formed with them reject the passive transformation. What is more relevant for us, however, is the fact that these same verbs resist the formation of a relative clause:

> * the teacher who he is
> * the salesman he became.

This feature, of course, provides an unexpected confirmation for our theory about the definite article: (37) and (38)

[63]

are discontinuous because the starting sentences cannot provide the clause for the subsequent *the* N-phrase.

Verbs accompanied by modal auxiliaries may or may not connect:

> (39) Joe can lift a bear
> (40) He could have married a rich girl
> (41) You must buy a house
> (42) I should have seen a play

remain ambiguous between generality and individuality concerning the second noun phrase.

In some cases nouns are identified by the mere presence of a verb in the past tense:

> A man caught a shark in a lake. The shark was a fully developed specimen.

2.18.   Finally, there is the least specific way of introducing a singular term:

> Once upon a time there was a king who had seven daughters. The king . . .

This pattern of "existential extraction" has great importance for us. It appears that it can be used as a criterion of identifying occurrence: a sentence is identifying with respect to an N if and only if the transform

> There is an N wh. . . . . .

is acceptable as a paraphrase. Thus the identifying sentences in (31)–(36) yield:

> There is a house I see.
> There is a hole they dug.
> There is a bone the dogs found.
> There is a snake that bit me.

There is a stick with which they dug a hole.
There is a boy who had dinner with me.

Nonidentifying sentences, like

A cat is an animal
A tiger eats meat

or the ones like (37)–(38), reject this form:

* There is an animal that is a cat.
* There is meat a tiger eats.
* There is a teacher he is.
* There is a salesman Joe became.

As for the modal sentences (39)–(42), it is obvious that the possibility of existential extraction is the sign of their being taken in the identifying sense:

There is a bear Joe can lift
There is a rich girl you could have married

and so on. We may conclude, then, that given any *the N wh. . . . . .*-phrase, it is a singular term if and only if the sentence *There is an N wh. . . . . .* is entailed by the discourse.

2.19. This conclusion should fill the hearts of all analytic philosophers with the glow of familiarity. Hence it may be worth while to review our conclusions from the point of view of recent controversies on the topic.

First of all we have found that the question whether or not a given *the N*-phrase is a singular term cannot be decided by considering only the sentence in which it occurs. Strawson's suggestion that it is the use of the sentence, or the expression, that is relevant is certainly true, but it falls short of telling us what it means to use a sentence to make a

[65]

statement, or to use a certain phrase to refer to something. Our results indicate a way of being more explicit and precise. At least with respect to *the* N-phrases, their being uniquely referring expressions, that is, singular terms, is conditioned by their occurrence in a discourse of a certain type. Such a discourse has to contain a previous sentence which identifies N, and, as we remember, such a sentence is always paraphraseable by the existential extraction, *There is an N wh. . . . . . .* Therefore, although Russell's claim, according to which sentences containing *the* N-type singular terms entail an assertion of existence, is too strong, Strawson's claim, that no such assertion is entailed by the referential occurrence of such a phrase is too weak. True, it is not the sentence containing the referential *the* N that entails the existential assertion, but another sentence, the occurrence of which, however, is a *conditio sine qua non* of a referential *the* N.

But, you object, the identifying sentence need not actually occur. In many cases it is merely assumed or presupposed. My answer is that this is philosophically irrelevant. The omission of the identifying sentence is a device of economy: we do not bother to state the obvious. What matters is the essential structure of the discourse. In giving a mathematical proof we often omit steps that are obvious to the audience, yet those steps remain part of the proof. The omission of the identifying sentence, like the omission of certain steps in a given proof, depends upon what the speaker deems to be obvious to the audience in question. And this has no philosophical significance.

Our conclusion is in accordance with common sense. If a child tells me

(43) The bear I shot yesterday was huge

I will answer

(44) But you did not shoot any bear.

(44) does not contradict (43). It contradicts, however, the sentence

(45) I shot a bear yesterday

which the child presupposed, but wisely omitted, in trying to get me to take *the bear* . . . as a referring expression. Is, then, (43) true or false? In itself it is neither, since the *the* N-phrase in it can achieve reference only if the preceding identifying sentence, (45), is true. Since this is not the case, *the bear* . . . fails to refer to anything in spite of the fact that it satisfies the conditions for a singular term.

Of course the logician, who abhors truth-gaps as nature does the void, will be justified in trying to unmask the impotence of such singular terms by insisting upon the inclusion of a version of the relevant identifying sentence (*There is an N wh.* . . . . .) into the analysis of sentences containing singular *the* N terms. In view of our results, this move is far less artificial than some authors have claimed.

2.20 The triumph of the partisans of the philosophical theory of descriptions will, however, be somewhat damped when we point out that sentences of the type

There is an N wh. . . . . .

do not necessarily assert "real" existence, let alone spatio-temporal existence. Take the following discourse:

I dreamt about a ship. The ship . . .

The identifying sentence easily yields the transform

There is a ship I dreamt about.

[67]

This may be true, yet it does not mean that there is such a ship in reality. If somebody suggests that that ship has a dream existence, or that the house I just imagined has an imaginary existence, or that the king with the seven daughters has a fairy-tale existence, I cannot but agree. I only add that it would be desirable to be able to characterize the various types of discourse appropriate to these kinds of "existence." Particularly, of course, we are interested in discourse pertaining to "real" existence. I give a hint. I remarked above that at the beginning of almost every discourse containing singular terms there must be a "basic" singular term (or its plural equivalent). Now if we find such a basic term denoting a real entity, like *I, Lyndon B. Johnson,* or *Uganda,* then we should trace the connection of other singular terms to these. As long as the links are formed by "reality-preserving" verbs like *push, kick,* and *eat,* we remain in spatio-temporal reality. Verbs like *dream, imagine, need, want, look for,* and *plan* should caution us: the link may be broken, although it need not be. Reality may enter by another path. If I only say

I dreamt about a house. The house . . .

one has no reason to think that the house I dreamt about is to be found in the world. If, however, I report

I dreamt about the house in which I was born. The house . . .

the house I talk about is a real house, but not by virtue of *dream* but by virtue of *being born in.* It is this latter and not the former verb that preserves reality. Of course, if the "basic" singular term is something like *Zeus,* or *the king who lived once upon a time,* the situation is clear.

The development of this hint would require much fascinating detail.

For the time being, we have to be satisfied with the conclusion that the discourse in which a referential *the N*-phrase occurs entails a *There is an N* . . . assertion. But we should add the *caveat:* there are things that do not really exist.

[3]

Each and Every, Any and All[1]

3.1 The universal quantifier, commonly represented as (x) (. . . x . . .), is used in symbolic logic to express general propositions. As indicated in the previous chapter, ordinary language has many devices to the same purpose. To mention affirmative forms only:

(1) *A tiger* is an animal.
(2) *Cats* love mice.
(3) *The viper* is a poisonous snake.
(4) *All men* are mortal.
(5) *Every paper* I read ran the story.
(6) *Each letter* I sent was intercepted.
(7) *Any doctor* will tell you what to do.

These devices are not freely interchangeable. Sentences like

* Any letter I sent was intercepted
Each cat loves mice

[1] This is a slightly expanded version of a paper, with the same title, which appeared in *Mind*, LXXI (1962), 145–160. Some paragraphs have been added from the article entitled "Any and All" in the *Encyclopedia of Philosophy* (ed. P. Edwards).

are deviant or odd, while the sentences

> A paper I read ran the story
> The letter I sent was intercepted

lack the generality of (5) and (6). No wonder, then, that in face of such linguistic complexities logicians hail the simplicity of technical notation. Even if it is not claimed that the theory can account for all the aspects that are involved in the correct use of these linguistic media, it is commonly maintained that the logically important features are well brought out, and taken care of in a manner that surpasses the original in clarity:

Quantification cuts across the vernacular use of 'all', 'every', 'any', and also 'some', 'a certain', etc., . . . in such a fashion as to clear away the baffling tangle of ambiguities and obscurities. . . . The device of quantification subjects this level of discourse, for the first time, to a clear and general algorithm.[2]

As the same text shows in detail, some ambiguities and obscurities are indeed cleared away by the technical devices at our disposal. Elated by this success one is naturally inclined to force all sentences in which these particles occur into the strait jacket prescribed by the theory of quantification, suppressing thereby, I fear, other aspects, among them logically important ones, that enter into the common understanding of these words. The fact that the theory has succeeded in clarifying some logically important points does not show that all the remaining points are of a mere stylistic but not logical interest; the fact that the cake once has been cut with success does not mean that this is the only profitable way of cutting the cake. More specifically, I have reasons to think that the method of lumping *each*, *every*, *all*, and *any* together and treating them as stylistic variants of

[2] W. V. Quine, *Mathematical Logic*, pp. 70–71.

[71]

the same logical structure tends to obscure issues concerning the type of reference, existential import, and lawlike form of general propositions. In the following, therefore, I shall attempt to discern and to exhibit the differences as well as the similarities in the role of these particles, which task, surprisingly enough, has never been undertaken yet in a systematic way, at least not to my knowledge.

3.2   As we consider the various sentences in which these particles occur, the first difference that strikes us is that *every* and *each* are always followed by the singular form of the noun, while *any* sometimes, and *all* nearly always, calls for the plural.

Leaving aside, for the time being, the less consistent *any*, we shall focus our attention on the difference in this respect between *all* on the one side, and *every* and *each* on the other, and we shall attempt to find the reason behind it. For, as we are going to see, it is by no means a mere caprice of grammar: it is indicative of a difference in the very meaning of these words.

Consider these propositions:

>   (8) All those blocks are yellow.
>   (9) All those blocks are similar.
>   (10) All those blocks fit together.
>   (11) The number of all those blocks is 17.

It is clear that (8) is true if and only if the proposition

>   (12) Each (every one) of those blocks is yellow

is true. Thus here, at least in so far as truth-values are concerned, no difference appears between the functions of these particles.

This, however, is obviously not the case in regard to (9), (10), and (11). For, to begin with,

Each (every one) of those blocks is similar

is an incomplete sentence; the question "Similar to what?" remains open. One may try to be more specific:

(13) Each of those blocks is similar to every other.

Even this version will not do though. If we interpret the relation of similarity as having at least one common characteristic, then it is quite possible that each block be similar to every other without all of them being similar. Nelson Goodman's example for an "imperfect community" is sufficient to illustrate the point.[3] Take three elements with characteristics distributed as follows: *ab, bc, ac*. Then, with the given interpretation, any two elements will be similar to each other without all of them being similar, since there is no common characteristic running through the total population. Thus while (9) obviously entails (13), the latter fails to entail the former.

As to (10), the difference is still more marked. There, again, the sentence

Each (every one) of those blocks fits together

does not make sense, and the improved version

(14) Each of those blocks fits every other

once more fails to amount to (9). It is quite possible that each block fits every other without all of them fitting together. Think of L-shaped blocks, any two fitting together to form a cube. Thus (14) does not entail (10). But, in this case, neither does (10), *per se*, entail (14): all the pieces of a jigsaw puzzle fit together without each piece fitting every other. Each, however, must fit some others.

Proposition (11) brings out the difference in the most extreme form. The counterpart sentence

[3] N. Goodman, *The Structure of Appearance*, p. 125.

>(15) The number of each (every one) of those
> blocks is 17

will not make sense unless an entirely different interpretation of *number of* is invoked—being marked, say, with the
numeral *17*. In which case, of course, there is no logical
relation between (11) and (15) whatever.

3.3. What do these examples show? We have found that
while in the case of a nonrelational predicate the difference
between the function of *all* and that of *every* and *each* did
not register in the truth-values of the propositions in which
they occurred, in the cases of certain relational predicates
that difference, as it were, could be exhibited in terms of
truth-values. Of course, exactly that was the point in using
these relational predicates. The relations of similarity (with
the given interpretation) and of fitting together can apply
to the whole set in a *collective* sense, or to subsets (couples)
of the whole group in a *distributive* sense; and the expressions *are similar* or *fit together* do not indicate, by themselves, in which of these senses they be predicated. It is,
therefore, up to the quantifier particles alone to decide the
issue. Since, however, the collective sense may fail to imply
the distributive sense and vice versa, that is to say, one respective proposition may be true and the other false, such
a difference in truth-values clearly indicates the difference
in the meaning of these particles. Similarly, in the last case,
the phrase *number of* requires an entirely different interpretation according to whether collective or distributive
reference is indicated by the quantifying particle. We can
safely conclude then that, at least with respect to a given
group of individuals, the reference appropriate to *all* is collective, and the reference appropriate to *each* or *every* is
distributive.

Proceeding from the other end we arrive at the same conclusion. Once more, for the given reason, relational predicates provide the best examples:

> Every member of the tribe has two wives
> Each item in the store costs $5

do not mean that all the members of the tribe (taken together) have only two wives, or that all the items in the store (taken together) are worth only $5. In all these cases, again, *all* implies collectivity, *every* or *each* distributivity.

Now we understand the reason why *all* calls for the plural, but *every* and *each* go with the singular. And we understand some other peculiarities as well. We mentioned above that while

> All those blocks are similar

is a complete sentence,

> Each (every one) of those blocks is similar

needs a complement. The reason is that similarity, being a relation, requires at least two terms; now *all*, with its collective reference, furnishes more than one already; *each* or *every*, being distributive, give us only one subject, though, as it were, many times over. No wonder, then, that we are looking for the other term(s): Similar to what?

Again, *all* has an exclusive and characteristic use in connection with nouns that are, in some sense or other, collective by themselves:

> All the information we obtained was worthless.
> All petroleum is organic in origin.
> All the nation remembered him.

We feel that the use of *all* is almost redundant here: it merely adds an emphasis to the universality of the subject.

[75]

Incidentally, such contexts are exceptions to the rule; here *all* goes with the singular.

Finally, the very possibility of phrases like *all together* and *all over* on the one hand, and *each separately* and *every single one* on the other, fits into the picture we succeeded in drawing by more elaborate means.

3.4. In the examples hitherto quoted we treated *every* and *each* pretty much alike. Yet, I think, a closer scrutiny reveals some differences here too. These, however, are much too fine to be located merely by comparing truth-values. In order to spot them we have to summon our best feeling for English idioms, and without disdaining help from other quarters, be they pragmatic or historical. In doing so, at appropriate junctions, I mean to cast a belated look on *all* as well; this might give us a chance of bringing some color into the logical sketch of the previous section.

Here, once more, we start off with a difference that is, in a sense, grammatical in nature. While the expression *each of them* is correct, *every of them* sounds ungrammatical; one has to say *every one of them*. On the contrary, *each one of them* is somewhat redundant. It looks as if *each* already implied *one* and drew our attention to the individual elements in a peculiar way. Indeed, while the sentences

> He came every day
> He came each day

are both correct (yet we feel some difference),

> He came each second day
> He came each three days

sound odd, the usual forms being

[76]

He came every second day
He came every three days.

The reason seems to be that no day is a second or a third day without a reference to other days. Now, then, while *every* considers the days as they are among other days, *each* takes them one by one, as it were without their environment. We may take a hint from the dictionaries, which tell us that *every* comes from *ever each;* thus originally it served to *sum up* the distribution characteristic of *each.* In this sense, *every* is between *each* and *all.* This explains why *every* becomes pompous if the reference class contains only two elements; we have to say

Each of the two . . .

instead of

Every one of the two . . .

Then it is not surprising to find an exclusive role for *each* in contexts like

Each in turn contributed his share.
They cost a penny each.
They love each other.
The sides of these triangles are equal each to each.

In the last two examples the role of *each* is more akin to that of *one* than to that of *every:* what we want to express is a one-to-one relation (*one another*) or correspondence (*one to one*).

Lest I should be accused of splitting hairs, I now shift my argument to more pragmatic grounds. Suppose I show you a basket of apples and I tell you

Take all of them.

If you started to pick them one by one, I should be surprised. My offer was sweeping: you should take the apples, if possible, "en bloc." Had I said

> Take every one of them

I should not care how you took them, provided you do not *leave* any behind. If I say

> Take each of them

one feels that the sentence is unfinished. Something like

> Take each of them and examine them in turn

is expected. Thus I expect you to take them one after the other not *missing* any.

The anticipated response to the first order squares nicely with the collective role of *all* we brought out in the previous section. The other two orders are both distributive, yet with a marked difference in emphasis: *every* stresses completeness or, rather, exhaustiveness (remember *ever each*); *each*, on the other hand, directs one's attention to the individuals as they appear, in some succession or other, one by one. Such an individual attention is not required in vain: you have to *do* something with each of them, one after the other.

It makes sense to say that all the deputies rose as the king entered the House (like *one man* they rose), it also makes sense to say that every one of them rose at that moment (*no one* remained seated), but it is rather queer to say that each of them rose at that moment. On the other hand, it is more proper to say that each deputy rose as his name was called than to say that every deputy rose as his name was called.

To summarize: our considerations in this section not only confirm the basic difference between the collective *all* and the distributive *every* and *each*, but they suggest a divergence in the respective functions of the last two particles as well. Moreover, as we have seen, some of these differences are not merely matters of grammar and style: they may affect truth-values as well. This result may encourage us to face our toughest but most important task: the examination of the logical behavior of *any*.

3.5 The meaning of *any* is a many-splendored thing. No example, in itself, could suffice to exhibit its wide variety of aspects. The best we can do is to discover these aspects one by one, isolate them, and then proceed to explain the import of *any* in some of its characteristic occurrences in terms of those aspects previously described.

As a first step, I take up the apple basket once more. Now I tell you

> Take any one of them.

This offer is far less generous than the previous ones: now I do not ask you to take all of them, every one of them, or each of them; I only give you one, though, for sure, the one you fancy. Thus there is some generosity left in this offer too: generosity in the sense of generality. Had I merely said

> Take one

you might test my good will by asking

> Do you mean *any* one?

Notice that it is not sufficient to say that the main feature of *any*, in such contexts, is the lack of determination. *Take one* lacks determination as well, but, and this is the crucial point, here the determination may still be up to me; you may sensibly ask back, *Which one?* With *Take any one*, it is up to you to do the determining; here it does not make sense to ask back, *Which one?* Thus while in the former case I merely fail to determine, in the latter case I call upon you to determine, in other words, I grant you the unrestricted liberty of individual choice. It is interesting to notice that the "tone" of freedom connoted by *any* excludes coercion: *Take any* is hardly an order; it is an offer. *I ordered (forced, compelled) him to take any* or *You must take any* hardly makes sense.

The point comes out still better in case of a claim or assertion. The assertion

> I can beat one of you

or

> I can beat some of you

does not amount, by a long shot, to the assertion

> I can beat any one of you.

The first two assertions claim that there is one person (or some persons) among you whom I can beat, but I do not care to indicate who he is (or who they are). The third, however, claims that no matter whom you select from among you, I can beat him.

For future reference, let us call this very peculiar aspect of the use of *any*, which, as we saw, succeeds in blending indetermination with generality, *freedom of choice*. This is an essential feature; so much so that in situations that exclude such freedom, the use of *any* becomes nonsensical. Suppose you accept my previous offer and take an apple. What can I say now? Well, for sure, I can say things like

> He took one
> He took the one he liked
> He took that one

but I certainly cannot say

    * He took any one

even if you acted on my words: *Take any one.* Thus, again, the main feature of *any* is not merely indetermination; for *He took one* is indeterminate enough. *Any* calls for a choice, but after it has been made *any* loses its point.

3.6. My original offer:

    Take any one of them

clearly restricted you as to the number of apples you were permitted to take. Nothing prevents me, however, from being more generous: I may tell you

    Take any two (three, etc.) of them.

Thus, it seems, *any*, by itself, is indifferent to the size of its immediate scope. This can be shown by another consideration too. If I ask you

    Did you take two?

and you took, say, three, you have to answer

    No, I took three.

If, on the other hand, my question is

    Did you take any?

you have to give an affirmative answer regardless of the number you took; you will say

    Yes, I took three.

This discloses, then, a new aspect of *any*, which we will call *indifference of size*. *Take any* leaves you free both as to which and how many to choose.

                   [81]

This indifference has a very curious limitation: if I formulate my offer in terms of *any*, there will be an upper limit to my generosity. In case the basket contains, for example, only five apples, I can go as far as to ask you to take any four of them, but I cannot, logically, go all the way and ask you to take any five of them. For to do so would render your freedom of choice vacuous and, consequently, my use of *any* senseless. Hence we may conclude that the immediate scope of *any* cannot exhaust the total population; in other words, *any* never amounts to *every*. Let us henceforth refer to this last property of our particle as its *incompleteness*.

3.7.   Now we are ready to examine some of the more interesting and more important uses of *any*. We hear, more often than we care to, commercials of the type:

Any doctor will tell you that Stopsneeze helps.

Suppose we are interested in commercial ethics and we want to check up on the sponsor's claim. How should we go about it?

"Well," you say, "obviously by finding out if it is indeed so." Unfortunately this answer, straightforward as it is, seems to call for something impossible. In order to realize this, I propose to consider two other examples first. Suppose you tell me

Dr. Jones will come tomorrow.

On the next day, after Dr. Jones has duly arrived, I can say

You told me that Dr. Jones would come today and he came indeed.

[82]

In other words, it happened as you predicted. Now suppose you say

> Dr. Jones will tell you that Stopsneeze helps.

This, too, may be taken as a simple forecast: he will tell me this whether I ask him or not. But the obvious sense is somewhat different: it amounts to

> If you ask Dr. Jones, he will tell you . . .

The prediction, in this case, is a conditional one. Now I ask Dr. Jones and he answers in the affirmative. Thus I conclude

> You predicted that if I ask Dr. Jones, he would tell me that Stopsneeze helps. I asked him and he indeed told me so.

In other words, again, it has turned out as you predicted. Finally we return to the sponsor's claim:

> Any doctor will tell you that Stopsneeze helps.

At the first sight, this seems to be a conditional forecast too:

> If you ask any doctor, he will tell you . . .

Now the question is how can I express a favorable result of my checking up on this claim? Well, I might end up with

> He said that any doctor would tell me that Stopsneeze helps. I asked Dr. Jones and he indeed told me so.

or

> . . . I asked a good many doctors and every one of them told me that Stopsneeze helps

but—and this is the crucial point—no matter what I did or what I learned, I shall not be able to say

> He said that any doctor would tell me that Stop-sneeze helps.* I asked any doctor(s), and he (they) told me the Stopsneeze helps.

Accordingly, in an important sense, I cannot conclude that what the sponsor said is indeed the case the way I could conclude in the previous examples.

What is the reason for this difference? If we recall what we said above about the freedom of choice of *any* then we realize that, though you can *ask* me to consult any doctor, or you can *claim* that any doctor will tell me such and such, I cannot *report* that I asked "any" doctor and I cannot *state* that "any" doctor told me such and such. The contexts *I asked x* and *x told me* are used to report a *fait accompli*, and such a use precludes the liberty of choice essential to *any*; facts are not free. You can state that *A* is *B* or that all the *A*'s are *B*, and after some investigation I may conclude, "I have inspected *A* and found it to be *B*" or "I have inspected all the *A*'s and found them to be *B*"; you can predict that *A* will be *B*, and in due time I may report, "*A* indeed has turned out to be *B*"; but, though you can claim that any *A* is *B*, I can never conclude, "I have seen any *A* and any *A* has turned out to be *B*."

> Ask Dr. Jones and he will tell you . . .

Here *he* refers to Dr. Jones.

> Ask any doctor and he will tell you . . .
> Ask any doctors and they will tell you . . .

Here *he* and *they* do not refer to "any" doctor or doctors that I may ask; they refer to the one or the ones I do ask.

And if I do not ask any? Then, I should say, they will not refer to anything at all. After all, the last two examples amount to

> Ask any doctor(s) and *the one(s) you ask* will tell you . . .

Thus it is I who has to supply the reference. To say

> Any doctor will tell you . . .

is to issue a *blank* warranty for conditional predictions: you fill in the names. You choose Dr. Jones; well, then *he* will tell you if you ask him. You pick twenty-five others; then, I say, *they* will tell you if you consult them. . . . If you do not ask any? In this case you do not use the blank; but it may be still good.

To sum up: in saying what he said the sponsor did not make a statement, which could be true or false. He did not make a prediction either, which could be correct or incorrect. What he did was to issue a blank warranty for conditional predictions, which may be reliable or not; he made a claim, which can be confirmed or disconfirmed, borne out or not borne out. In a sense, he offered a challenge to us, which we may take up or not. Much the same way as *Take any* is not an order, which is obeyed or disobeyed, but an offer, which is accepted or declined.

3.8.   Having thus put myself way out on a limb, I may expect the objection: "This is sheer sophistry; what the sponsor said is true if every doctor agrees that Stopsneeze helps, otherwise it is false."

My reply is that you are unfair to our sponsor—for he did *not* claim that. Moreover, honest as he is, he would not make a claim that cannot be substantiated. For one thing, who can be sure that there will never be a doctor who would think otherwise? His claim, however, can be substantiated: you may select the doctor you can trust, you may consult as many as you please, and if none of these disagrees, then you may conclude that the sponsor's claim holds water.

"You are lax," you insist; "*I* should not quit till I had asked every doctor in the world."

Now you are not only unfair but illogical as well. The sponsor, in effect, challenged you to select any doctor, or doctors—ask them and they will tell you. . . . And now you want to select *all* of them, which, of course, is more than impolite. Remember the apples. I said "Take any." Do you want to suggest that short of taking all you did not accept the offer? No, I say, taking all would be an abuse of it. Your requirement of completeness clashes, once more, with the freedom of choice of *any*.

"But then," you ask, "what would amount to a confirmation of the sponsor's claim according to you?"

As I just said: I should ask a good many doctors, very conscientious specialists among them, and if their verdict is uniformly favorable (or, perhaps, *almost* uniformly favorable), then I should conclude that the sponsor's claim is confirmed, otherwise not. In other words, I should exercise the freedom of choice granted me by the use of *any* in selecting doctors I trust; I should take advantage of the indifference of size of the same particle in consulting as many as I please; but, finally, I should not feel obliged to run through the space-time universe in an interminable search for all the doctors in it, thanks to the incompleteness entailed by the very same particle. If you prefer to call this an incomplete verification, be happy with it; I only remind you that the idea of a complete verification is repugnant to an *any*-proposition.

[86]

3.9. We noted above that the claim

Any doctor will tell you that Stopsneeze helps

is by no means discredited if as a matter of fact *no* doctor tells me that Stopsneeze helps, simply because I do not ask any. In a similar way the bylaw

Anybody trespassing on the premises will be prosecuted

will not be rendered false even if no one ever enters the premises. Such a lack of "existential import" is not limited to rules, regulations, bylaws, or propositions formulated in the future tense. Compare:

Every one of my friends smokes a pipe.
Anybody who is my friend smokes a pipe.

The first proposition would be senseless if I had no friends. Not so the second. It means that if somebody is my friend, he smokes a pipe; if he does not, he is not my friend; and I do not make exceptions, no matter who be the person. Then it is quite possible that I have no friends. It is not even surprising.
Consider, too, propositions of the sort:

Any nation that conquers the moon can control the earth.
Any perpetual-motion engine would violate the laws of thermodynamics, which is impossible.

It is obvious that we may accept these propositions even though we know that no nation has yet conquered the moon, or, in the second case, even though we imply that there never will be a perpetual-motion engine. After all, one might say things like

> Anybody who could do that would perform a
> miracle

even if one does not believe in miracles.

Thus, in terms of the previous analogy, the blank warranty issued for conditional predictions, or, for that matter, conditional statements, may contain such specifications in the antecedent that nothing actually does or nothing can qualify for it, nothing does or nothing can fill the bill. But then, one may ask, what is the point of making such an empty claim; what is the use of a cheque that cannot be cashed? Empty as it is, I reply, such a bill is not given in vain. On the strength of the first proposition one may arrive at the sobering conclusion:

> If Russia were to conquer the moon, she could control the earth.

And, on the basis of the second, one may rebut the would-be inventor:

> If your contraption were a perpetual-motion engine, it would violate the laws of thermodynamics, which is impossible.

In this second case we argue exactly from the impossibility of the consequent to that of the antecedent.

The importance, therefore, of an *any*-proposition does not consist in the actual fulfillment of the conditions mentioned in the antecedent and the consequent, but in the very relation of these conditions. Such a proposition amounts to the claim that any object fulfilling the condition specified by the antecedent is subject to the condition spelled out by the consequent: if a thing satisfies the former, it will satisfy the latter too; or, at least, if a thing were subject to the first, it would be subject to the second as well.

Once more, the *any*-proposition is an unrestricted warranty for conditional statements or forecasts and, we may add, for contrary-to-fact conditionals. In other words, to draw an obvious conclusion, it is an open hypothetical, a lawlike assertion.[4]

3.10. In discussing the differences between *all, every,* and *each,* at the beginning of our investigations, the examples were selected in such a way that the range of the quantifying particle was clearly restricted, by a suitable pronoun or identifying clause, to a definite and finite set of objects: a group of blocks, a basket of apples, and so on. Later, while considering *any,* we encountered examples of a different sort: they mentioned doctors, trespassers, perpetual-motion engines, and so on, in a rather indefinite way; to put it roughly we did not really refer to a set of such individuals, but we focused our attention on the condition of being a doctor, a trespasser, or what not, and on the consequences of fulfilling that condition for no matter what individual. Accordingly, the proposition did not presume to identify the candidates; in this respect it remained indefinite and open. To use a simile: we were not interested in the fish caught in the net, but in the net that might catch certain fish; and we were not disturbed if, in fact, it did not catch any.

This shift in the nature of our examples gives us a hint toward a sharper formulation of a distinction that sets *any* wide apart from *each* and *every,* and splits the use of *all* right in the middle.

We begin by considering two types of sentence we neglected hitherto: questions and negations. It is quite clear that the questions

---

[4] G. Ryle recognizes the connection between the use of *any* and lawlikeness (*The Concept of Mind,* pp. 120 ff.).

> Did you see all the pigs in the pen?
> Did you see every pig in the pen?

presuppose that there were pigs in the pen. In much the same way the negatives

> I did not see all the pigs in the pen
> I did not see every pig in the pen

imply that there were some pigs in the pen the speaker did not see, and strongly suggest that he has seen some. The same point holds, in suitable contexts, for *each* too: the question and answer

> Did you reply to each letter?
> I did not reply to each letter

would be out of place if no letters had been received. *Any*, on the other hand, does not indicate existential import:

> Did you see any pigs in the pen?
> I did not see any pigs in the pen

do not require any pigs in the pen. Moreover, explicit questions of existence, like

> Are there any pigs in the pen?

take full advantage of the existential neutrality of *any*.

The same point is reinforced by considering affirmative contexts.

> Each (every) message you sent was intercepted

is a correct sentence, but

> Each (every) message you might have sent would have been intercepted

is certainly not. *Any* works the opposite way:

[90]

> Any messages you might have sent would have been
> intercepted

is the correct sentence, and

> *Any messages you sent were intercepted

is the incorrect one. Thus, again, *each* and *every* are at home in existential contexts, while *any* sits pretty in non-existential ones. *All*, in this case, has a surprise in store:

> All the messages you sent were intercepted
> All messages you might have sent would have been
> intercepted

are both acceptable in spite of the obvious lack of existential import in the second proposition.

We have to say, therefore, that while *each* and *every* always connote existence, *all*, by itself, does not. It may occur, however, as we have seen in earlier examples, in propositions that do have existential import due to some other referential device which may be joined to *all* within the same noun phrase (definite article, demonstrative or possessive pronoun, etc.). This possibility is not available with *any:* we do not have *any the . . .* , *any my . . .* , etc. We have to say, for example, *any one of the . . .* — that is, we put the definite article into a separate noun phrase which then will carry existential import.

Any and *all*, then, share a common feature: they may occur in constructions lacking definite reference and existential import and, we may add, in this case they occur in the same sense. For, to quote a few examples, in

> All messages you might have sent . . .
> Any messages you might have sent . . .

or

> Try to do it by all means
> Try to do it by any means

or

> All violations will be prosecuted
> Any violation will be prosecuted

all and *any* may indeed be said to be but stylistic variants. And, naturally, none of these occurrences can be supplanted by *each* or *every* without producing a somewhat odd specimen.

Thus *any* and *all* are related and *each* and *every* are related. This is beautifully brought out by the fact that we have two combined forms: *any and all* and *each and every*. It is rewarding to look at them for a moment. Consider

> Each and every letter has been returned
> Any and all letters will be returned.

We feel that *every* and *all* merely serve here to add an emphasis to the appropriate universality of *each* and *any*. But then, of course, the import of such nonexistential *all* cannot be different from that of *any*, as the import of *every* is basically the same as that of *each*. Remember, *every* is *ever each*. Is such an *all*, then, something like *ever any?* This we do not have, but we have *whatever* (and its kin: *whenever*, *wherever*, etc.). A little reflection shows that the latter, again, is related to *any*, rather than to *each* or *every*.

3.11. One of the most surprising features of the use of *any* is the curious restriction that prohibits its occurrence in simple declarative sentences:

> *Any doctor told me . . .
> *I asked any doctor . . .

[92]

are ungrammatical and even

> Any raven is black

is somewhat deviant. In this last case we can correct the situation by introducing a modal clause:

> Any raven you may select will be black.

Now *all* is more liberal in this respect. We do not need clauses or modalities to form the correct sentence:

> All ravens are black.

Yet, the import of such a nonreferential use of *all* is similar to that of the nonreferential *any*. First, it is existentially neutral:

> All bodies not acted upon by external forces . . .

There are no such bodies. Nevertheless the law is important and fertile. For one thing, it warrants counterfactual inferences like

> If this body were not acted upon by external forces, then it would . . .

Second, just as I can claim that any doctor *will* tell you what to do, but cannot state that any doctor *did* tell you what to do, so I can also claim that all ravens *are* black, but cannot state that all raven *were* black. The best I can do is to say

> All the ravens we inspected were black

which is the same as

> Each (every) raven we inspected was black.

Thus the nonreferential *all*-proposition, in much the same way as the nonreferential *any*-proposition, cannot be found true as a result of an enumerative induction. Such propositions always remain open, whereas statements of evidence, statements of fact, are necessarily closed. Laws are not statements of fact and statements of fact are not laws. Consequently, *all* jumps into the breach to carry the logical import of *any* in simple declarative contexts, where *any*, owing to its linguistic constraints, would be out of place. And the result is the standard form of a scientific law.

We just said that such laws cannot be verified in a straightforward sense. This, however, does not mean that they cannot be confirmed. And it is exactly in view of their confirmation that the affinity of *all* to *any* rather than to *every* or *each* becomes crucial.

3.12.   In order to show this I propose a finite model. A bag contains a hundred marbles. We inspect ten at random and all ten are red. Then the probability that any one marble we care to pick out of the hundred will be red is quite high. Yet the probability of every one's being red is much lower.[5] If the bag contains a thousand marbles, then, given the same evidence, the probability of the latter proposition becomes still lower, while that of the former will hardly change. And, obviously, if the number of marbles approaches infinity, the probability of the *every*-proposition approaches zero, but the probability of the *any*-proposition remains substantially the same. Now, let us suppose that our evidence is mixed: we found nine red marbles and one black

[5] Nicod notices this relation. "If it is probable that *all* the A's are B, it is even more probable that *any* A is B, for then we have only one risk instead of several. On the other hand, when it is probable that *any* A is B, it may at the same time be improbable and even impossible that *all* the A's are B. This is what happens when it is certain or probable that there is, for instance, only one A out of a thousand that is not B" (J. Nicod, *Foundations of Geometry and Induction*, p. 211).

marble. The *any*-proposition still retains a fair probability, but the probability of the *every*-proposition will be zero. Any acceptable theory of probability would agree with these intuitive conclusions.

It follows that if the law

(16) All ravens are black

is taken in the sense of

(17) Every raven in the universe is black

then, no matter how large is our evidence, the law's probability will stay close to zero in view of the near infinity of ravens, past, present, and future. If, however, (16) is interpreted as

(18) Any raven we may select will be black

then, given the actual evidence, its probability will be high regardless of the size of the universe and the number of ravens in it. Moreover, although an albino raven makes (17) plainly false, the probability of (18) will be only slightly affected. I may add that the scope of (18) can be extended to any two, three, and so on, as far as we care to go; ample evidence will support us in taking larger risks.

Considering the actual practice of science it is quite clear that its *all*-propositions are interpreted in the sense of *any* rather than that of *every*. Professor Carnap recognizes this in proposing "qualified-instance-confirmation" as the true measure of confirmation for inductive laws.[6]

[6] R. Carnap, *Logical Foundations of Probability*, pp. 571 ff. "When he [the engineer] says that the law is very reliable, he does not mean to say that he is willing to bet that among the billion of billions, or an infinite number, of instances to which the law applies there is not one counterinstance, but merely that this bridge will not be a counterinstance, or that among all bridges he will construct during his lifetime there will be no counterinstance" (*ibid.*, p. 572).

However this may be, our results are sufficient to show that a simple application of the theory of quantification may fall short of capturing all the logically relevant features involved in the vernacular use of the particles of quantification. Some such features can already be found by contrasting *all* with *each* and *every*, but the most important points missed by the theory are the ones that emerge in connection with *any*. For we have reasons to hope that a close analysis of the use of this last particle, together perhaps with corresponding logical models, might open up a new line of attack on the problem of lawlike propositions. And in these matters a hope is an achievement.

[4]

Verbs and Times[1]

4.1. The fact that verbs have tenses indicates that considerations involving the concept of time are relevant to their use. These considerations are not limited merely to the obvious discrimination between past, present, and future; there is another, a more subtle dependence on that concept: the use of a verb may also suggest the particular way in which that verb presupposes and involves the notion of time.

In a number of recent publications some attention has been paid to these finer aspects, perhaps for the first time systematically. Distinctions have been made among verbs suggesting processes, states, dispositions, occurrences, tasks, achievements, and so on. Obviously these differences cannot be explained in terms of time alone: other factors, like the presence or absence of an object, conditions, intended states of affairs, also enter the picture. Nevertheless one

[1] With only minor changes this chapter reproduces an article of the same title which appeared in *The Philosophical Review*, LXVI (1957), 143–160.

feels that the time element remains crucial; at least it is important enough to warrant separate treatment. Indeed, as I intend to show, if we focus our attention primarily upon the time schemata presupposed by various verbs,[2] we are able to throw light on some of the obscurities which still remain in these matters. These time schemata will appear as important constituents of the concepts that prompt us to use those terms the way we consistently do.

There are a few such schemata of very wide application. Once they have been discovered in some typical examples, they may be used as models of comparison in exploring and clarifying the behavior of any verb whatever.

In indicating these schemata, I do not claim that they represent all possible ways in which verbs can be used correctly with respect to time determination nor that a verb exhibiting a use fairly covered by one schema cannot have divergent uses, which in turn may be described in terms of the other schemata. As a matter of fact, precisely those verbs that call for two or more time schemata will provide the most interesting instances of conceptual divergence in this respect—an ambiguity which, if undetected, might lead to confusion. Thus my intention is not to give rules about how to use certain terms but to suggest a way of describing the use of those terms. I shall present some *"objects of comparison* which are meant to throw light on the facts of our language by way not only of similarities, but also of dissimilarities . . . a measuring rod; not as a preconceived idea to which reality *must* correspond."[3]

4.2. Our first task therefore will be to locate and to describe the most common time schemata implied by the use

[2] I am aware of my duty to explain what exactly I mean by *time schema* in this context. I shall do so in due course.

[3] L. Wittgenstein, *Philosophical Investigations*, I, 130–131.

of English verbs. To do this I need some clear-cut examples which, at least in their dominant use, show forth these schemata in pure form. At this stage, I shall try to avoid ambiguous terms and ignore stretched and borderline uses.

I start with the well-known difference between verbs that possess continuous tenses and verbs that do not. The question

> What are you doing?

might be answered by

> I am running (or writing, working, and so on)

but not by

> I am knowing (or loving, recognizing, and so on).[4]

On the other hand, the appropriate question and answer

> Do you know . . . ?
> Yes, I do

have no counterparts like

> Do you run?
> Yes, I do.[5]

This difference suggests that running, writing, and the like are processes going on in time, that is, roughly, that they consist of successive phases following one another in time. Indeed, the man who is running lifts up his right leg one moment, drops it the next, then lifts his other leg, drops it, and so on. But although it can be true of a subject that he knows something at a given moment or for a certain period, knowing and its kin are not processes going on in

[4] The presence or absence of an object is irrelevant here. *I am pushing a cart* is a correct sentence, while *I am loving you* remains nonsense.

[5] Unless a very different meaning of *running* is involved, which I shall discuss later.

[99]

time. It may be the case that I know geography now, but this does not mean that a process of knowing geography is going on at present consisting of phases succeeding one another in time.

First let us focus our attention on the group of verbs that admit continuous tenses. There is a marked cleavage within the group itself. If it is true that someone is running or pushing a cart now, then even if he stops in the next moment it will be still true that he did run or did push a cart. On the other hand, even if it is true that someone is drawing a circle or is running a mile now, if he stops in the next moment it may not be true that he did draw a circle or did run a mile.[6] In other words, if someone stops running a mile, he did not run a mile; if one stops drawing a circle, he did not draw a circle. But the man who stops running did run, and he who stops pushing the cart did push it. Running a mile and drawing a circle have to be finished, while it does not make sense to talk of finishing running or pushing a cart. Thus we see that while running or pushing a cart has no set terminal point, running a mile and drawing a circle do have a "climax," which has to be reached if the action is to be what it is claimed to be.

Accordingly, the question

For how long did he push the cart?

is a significant one, while

How long did it take to push the cart?

sounds odd. On the other hand

[6] For a clear formulation of this criterion see S. Bromberger's "An Approach to Explanation" in R. J. Butler (ed.), *Analytical Philosophy*, second series, pp. 72–105. Bromberger correctly points out an error I committed in giving this criterion in the original paper (pp. 74–75).

How long did it take to draw the circle?

is the appropriate question, and

For how long did he draw the circle?

is somewhat queer. And, of course, the corresponding answers will be

He was pushing it for half an hour

and

It took him twenty seconds to draw the circle

or

He did it in twenty seconds

and not vice versa. Pushing a cart may go on for a time, but it does not take any definite time; the activity of drawing may also go on for a time, but it takes a certain time to draw a circle.

A very interesting consequence follows. If it is true that someone has been running for half an hour, then it must be true that he has been running for every period within that half hour. But even if it is true that a runner has run a mile in four minutes, it cannot be true that he has run a mile in any period which is a real part of that time, although it remains true that he was running, or that he was engaged in running a mile, during any substretch of those four minutes. Similarly, in case I wrote a letter in an hour, I did not write it, say, in the first quarter of that hour. It appears, then, that running and its kind go on in time in a homogeneous way; any part of the process is of the same nature as the whole. Not so with running a mile or writing a letter; they also go on in time, but they proceed toward a terminus which is logically necessary to their being what they are.

[101]

Somehow this climax casts its shadow backward, giving a new color to all that went before.

Thus we have arrived at the time schemata of two important species of verb. Let us call the first type, that of *running, pushing a cart,* and so forth, "activity terms," and the second type, that of *running a mile, drawing a circle,* and so forth, "accomplishment terms." [7] The description of these first two categories also illustrates what I mean by exhibiting the "time schemata" of verbs.

When one turns to the other genus, that is, to the verbs lacking continuous tenses, one discovers a specific difference there too. As we said above, verbs like *knowing* and *recognizing* do not indicate processes going on in time, yet they may be predicated of a subject for a given time with truth or falsity. Now some of these verbs can be predicated only for single moments of time (strictly speaking), while others can be predicated for shorter or longer periods of time. One reaches the hilltop, wins the race, spots or recognizes something, and so on at a definite moment. On the other hand, one can know or believe something, love or dominate somebody, for a short or long period. The form of pertinent questions and answers proves the point neatly:

> At what time did you reach the top? At noon sharp.
> At what moment did you spot the plane? At 10:53
> A.M.

but

[7] In the absence of a "pure" terminology I am forced to be content with these names (and the other two to be given), which also connote aspects beyond time structure (e.g., that of success). If we do not forget that our point of view is limited to time schemata, however, we shall not be surprised when, for example, *getting exhausted* turns out to be an accomplishment term and *dying* an achievement term in our sense.

> For how long did you love her? For three years.
> How long did you believe in the stork? Till I was
> seven.

and not the other way around.[8]

Before going any further let us call the first family (that
of *reaching the top*) "achievement terms," and the second
(that of *loving*) "state terms." Then we can say that
achievements occur at a single moment, while states last for
a period of time.

4.3.   Our conclusion about achievements is reinforced by
a curious feature pointed out by Gilbert Ryle (following
Aristotle), namely that "I can say 'I have seen it' as soon as
I can say 'I see it.' "[9] As a matter of fact the point can be
made stronger still: in cases of pure achievement terms the
present tense is almost exclusively used as historic present
or as indicating immediate future:

> Now he finds the treasure (or wins the race, and so
> on)

is not used to report the actual finding or winning, while
the seemingly paradoxical

> Now he has found it

or

> At this moment he has won the race

is.

The fact that we often say things like

[8] Even in *I knew it only for a moment* the use of *for* indicates
that a period, though very short, is to be understood.

[9] *Dilemmas*, p. 102. He quotes Aristotle's *Met.* 1048b. As we shall
see later, this particular example is a bit misleading.

> It took him three hours to reach the summit
> He found it in five minutes

might tempt a novice to confuse achievements (which belong to the second genus) with accomplishments (which belong to the first). A little reflection is sufficient to expose the fallacy. When I say that it took me an hour to write a letter (which is an accomplishment), I imply that the writing of the letter went on during that hour. This is not the case with achievements. Even if one says that it took him three hours to reach the summit, one does not mean that the "reaching" of the summit went on during those hours.[10] Obviously it took three hours of climbing to reach the top. Put in another way: if I write a letter in an hour, then I can say

> I am writing a letter

at any time during that hour; but if it takes three hours to reach the top, I cannot say

> I am reaching the top

at any moment of that period.

As to states, the lack of continuous tenses (e.g., *I am knowing, loving,* and so forth) is enough to distinguish them from activities and accomplishments, and the form of time determination (*How long . . . ? For such and such a period*) should be sufficient to keep them from being confused with achievements.

Still, I think it might be useful to mention, by way of digression, a surprising feature about states which is not strictly connected with considerations of time.

When I say that I could run if my legs were not tied, I

[10] For those who like oddities: *It took the battalion twenty minutes to cross the border; They are crossing the border.* Such are the borderline cases I mean to ignore at this stage.

do not imply that I *would* run if my legs were not tied. On the other hand, there is a sense of *can* in which

He could know the answer if he had read Kant

does mean that in that case he *would* know the answer. Similarly, in an obvious sense, to say that I could like her if she were not selfish is to say that I would like her if she were not selfish. One feels something strange in

Even if I could like her I would not like her.

It appears, therefore, that in conditionals *could* is often interchangeable with *would* in connection with states. For the same reason, *can* might become redundant in indicative sentences of this kind. Hence the airy feeling about *I can know, I can love, I can like,* and so forth. This also explains why *I can believe it* is very often used instead of *I believe it.* And, to anticipate, the question *Do you see the rabbit?* can be answered equivalently by *Yes, I can see it* or *Yes, I see it.* Later on, in connection with a concrete example, I shall take up this matter again and try to be more specific. For the present, it is enough to mention that while to be able to run is never the same thing as to run or to be able to write a letter is by no means the same as to write it, it seems to be the case that, in some sense, to be able to know is to know, to be able to love is to love, and to be able to see is to see.

One might point out that some achievements also share this feature. Indeed, in some sense, to be able to recognize is to recognize and to be able to spot the plane is to spot the plane. On the other hand, to be able to start or stop running is by no means the same thing as to start or stop running, although to start or to stop running are clearly achievements according to their time schema. Thus here the con-

[105]

sideration of the time element is not sufficient; we have to look for another criterion. If we consider that one can start or stop running deliberately or carefully and also that one can be accused of, or held responsible for, having started or stopped running but not of having spotted or recognized something, then we realize that the above-mentioned curious behavior with respect to *can* is proper to verbs denoting achievements that cannot be regarded as voluntary (or involuntary) actions.

Following this lead back to states, we find indeed that one cannot know, believe, or love deliberately or carefully, and none of us can be accused of, or held responsible for, having "done" so either.[11] We may conclude this digression by saying that states and some achievements cannot be qualified as actions at all.[12]

By way of illustration to this section, I add four examples which demonstrate our time schemata from another angle.

For activities: *A was running at time t* means that time instant *t* is on *a* time stretch throughout which *A* was running.

For accomplishments: *A was drawing a circle at t* means that *t* is on *the* time stretch in which *A* drew that circle.

For achievements: *A won a race between t_1 and t_2* means that *the* time instant at which *A* won that race is between t_1 and t_2.

For states: *A loved somebody from t_1 to t_2* means that at *any* instant between t_1 and t_2 *A* loved that person.

This shows that the concept of activities calls for periods of time that are not unique or definite. Accomplishments,

[11] They are not "done" or "performed" at all.

[12] In my remarks on *can*, and in taking *deliberately* and *carefully* as criteria for genuine actions, I have made use of my (not very trustworthy) recollection of J. L. Austin's lectures given at Harvard in 1955.

on the other hand, imply the notion of unique and definite time periods. In an analogous way, while achievements involve unique and definite time instants, states involve time instants in an indefinite and nonunique sense.

This division has an air of completeness about it. Perhaps it is more than a mere presumption to think that all verbs can be analyzed in terms of these four schemata.

4.4. Having thus formed and polished our conceptual tools, in the following sections I shall try to show how they can be used in practice. Here, of course, it would be foolish to claim any completeness: all I can do is to make some remarks on a few verbs or groups of verbs and hope that the reader, if he deems it worth while, will be able to proceed to other verbs in which he is interested.

There is a very large number of verbs that fall completely, or at least in their dominant use, within one of these categories.[13] A little reflection shows that running, walking, swimming, pushing or pulling something, and the like are almost unambiguous cases of activity. Painting a picture, making a chair, building a house, writing or reading a novel, delivering a sermon, giving or attending a class, playing a game of chess, and so forth, as also growing up, recovering from illness, getting ready for something, and so on, are clearly accomplishments. Recognizing, realizing, spotting and identifying something, losing or finding an object, reaching the summit, winning the race, crossing the border, starting, stopping, and resuming something, being born, and even dying fall squarely into the class of achievements. Having, possessing, desiring, or wanting something, liking, disliking, loving, hating, ruling, or dominating somebody

---

[13] For the sake of stylistic simplicity I shall, in what follows, be somewhat casual with respect to the "use versus mention" of verbs.

or something, and, of course, knowing or believing things are manifestly states.

In connection with the last group, an obvious idea emerges. From the point of view of time schemata, being married, being present or absent, healthy or ill, and so on also behave like states. But then we can take one more step and realize that this is true of all qualities. Indeed, something is hard, hot, or yellow for a time, yet to be yellow, for instance, does not mean that a process of yellowing is going on. Similarly, although hardening is a process (activity or accomplishment), being hard is a state. Now perhaps we understand why desiring, knowing, loving, and so on—the so-called immanent operations of traditional philosophy—can be and have been looked upon as qualities.

Habits (in a broader sense including occupations, dispositions, abilities, and so forth) are also states in our sense. Compare the two questions: *Are you smoking?* and *Do you smoke?* The first one asks about an activity, the second, a state. This difference explains why a chess player can say at all times that he plays chess and why a worker for the General Electric Company can say, while sunbathing on the beach, that he works for General Electric.

It is not only activities that are "habit-forming" in this sense. Writers are people who write books or articles, and writing a book is an accomplishment; dogcatchers are men who catch dogs, and catching a dog is an achievement.

Now the curious thing is that while cabdrivers—that is, people of whom one can always say that they drive a cab—sometimes are actually driving a cab, rulers—that is, people of whom one can always say that they rule a country—are never actually ruling a country, that is, they are never engaged in a specific activity of ruling a country comparable to the specific activity of driving a cab. A cabdriver might say that he was driving his cab all morning, but the king of Cambodia can hardly say that he was ruling Cambodia all morning. The obvious explanation is that while driving a cab is a fairly uniform thing, as are also smoking, painting, and writing, the actions which a ruler as such is supposed to perform are manifold and quite disparate in nature.[14] Is he "ruling" only while he is addressing the assembly and surveying troops, or also while he is eating lobster at a state dinner? We feel that some of his actions are more appropriate than others to his state as a ruler, but we also feel that none of them in particular can be called "ruling." Of course, a painter also performs diverse actions which are more or less related to his profession (e.g., watching the sunset or buying canvas); nevertheless there is one activity, actually painting, which is "the" activity of a painter.

Adopting Ryle's terminology,[15] I shall call the states of smokers, painters, dogcatchers, and the like *specific* states, and the states of rulers, servants, educators (and grocers, who not only are never actually "grocing" but also do not "groce": the verb *groce* does not happen to exist) *generic* states.

This much it has seemed necessary to say about states, that puzzling category in which the role of verb melts into that of predicate, and actions fade into qualities and relations.

4.5. As we see, the distinction between the activity sense and the state sense of *to smoke, to paint*, and the like is a general distinction, not peculiar to the concept of smoking or painting alone. Many activities (and some accomplishments and achievements) have a "derived" state sense.

---

[14] As pointed out by Ryle in *The Concept of Mind*, pp. 44, 118.
[15] *Ibid.*, p. 118.

There is, however, a group of verbs with conceptual divergences of their own. With respect to many of these verbs, it is hardly possible to establish the category to which they "originally" belong. The group of verbs I have in mind comprises philosophically notorious specimens like *to think, to know, to understand,* on the one hand, and *to see, to hear,* and their kindred on the other.[16] In recent years a number of excellent publications have succeeded in pointing out that the alleged epistemological problems surrounding this family look far less formidable when we become aware of the mistakes of category that are embedded in their very formulation; one can hardly state the problem so long as one refuses to talk incorrect English.

I venture to claim that our categories, based upon time schemata, not only do justice to these recent discoveries but, beyond that, can be employed in exposing and eliminating certain mistakes and oversimplifications which are apt to discredit the whole method. Let us begin with *thinking.* It is clear that it is used in two basic senses. *Thinking* functions differently in

He is thinking about Jones

and in

He thinks that Jones is a rascal.

The first "thinking" is a process, the second a state. The first sentence can be used to describe what one is doing; the second cannot. This becomes obvious when we consider that while

[16] We shall see that, although knowing remains quite a typical state, at this point it deserves another look.

[110]

He thinks that Jones is a rascal

might be said truthfully of someone who is sound asleep

He is thinking about Jones

cannot. It shows that thinking about something is a process that goes on in time, an activity one can carry on deliberately or carefully, but this is by no means true of thinking that something is the case. If it is true that he was thinking about Jones for half an hour, then it must be true that he was thinking about Jones during all parts of that period. But even if it is true that he thought that Jones was a rascal for a year, that does not necessarily mean that he was thinking about Jones, the rascal, for any minute of that time.

The last fact shows that *thinking that* is not related to *thinking about* the way *smoking* in its habit sense is related to *smoking* in its activity sense. *Thinking that* is rather like *ruling*, that is, it is based upon actions of various kinds. Consider the behavior of the farmer who thinks that it is going to rain. We may say, then, that *thinking that* is a generic state. On the other hand, the state of a "thinker" is a specific state: he is a man who is very often engaged in thinking about ponderous matters.[17]

It is easy to see that *believing that* is also a generic state. As a matter of fact, *he believes that* can be exchanged for *he thinks that* in most cases. *Believing in*, though different in meaning, belongs to the same category; one can believe in the right cause even while asleep.

Knowing is clearly a state in its dominant uses (*knowing that, knowing how, knowing something* [*somebody*]). Fur-

---

[17] I am in doubt about *thinking of something*. Its use is not steady enough. It seems to me, though, that very often it has an achievement sense: *Every time I see that picture I think of you.*

thermore, since *I am knowing* does not exist in English, knowing seems to be a generic state. For example, the fact that I know that Harvard is in Cambridge is behind a host of my actions that range from addressing letters to boarding buses. Yet none of these actions in particular can be qualified as *knowing*. Doubts might arise, however, from uses like *And then suddenly I knew!* and *Now I know it!* which sound like achievements. Indeed, this insight sense of knowing fits more or less into that category. Yet it would be a mistake to think that this kind of *knowing* is related to the state sense in the way that catching dogs is related to the specific state of dogcatchers. A little reflection shows that they are related rather as getting married (achievement) is to being married (generic state). This is best shown in an example. Suppose someone is trying to solve a problem in mathematics. Suddenly he cries out "Now I know it!" After ten minutes he explains the solution to me. Obviously he still knows it, which means that no flashes of understanding are necessary for him to explain it. Indeed, so long as he knows it (in a state sense), it is logically impossible that he will "know" it (in an achievement sense). *Now I know it!* indicates that he did not know it before.

One is tempted here to say that "knowing" means to start knowing. This is a dangerous temptation; it makes us think that just as to start running begins the activity of running, to start knowing begins the activity of knowing. Of course, the fact that *to start* (*or to stop*) *knowing* does not make sense demonstrates that "knowing" is not the beginning of an activity but the beginning of a state. In general, it is important to distinguish achievements that start activities from achievements that initiate a state.

The same distinctions hold for *understanding*. Its achievement sense, however, is perhaps more common than that of

knowing; we have just now mentioned "flashes" of understanding. But these flashes of understanding are also achievements initiating the generic state of understanding.

4.6.   We must keep in mind all these subtleties as we proceed to the arduous task of analyzing the concept of *seeing*
from the point of view of temporal structure. In *The Concept of Mind* [18] and also in *Dilemmas* [19] Ryle quite consistently maintains that seeing is not a process nor a state but
a kind of achievement or success, in many respects similar
to winning a race or finding something. More recently F.
N. Sibley has pointed out that in a number of its significant
uses, *seeing* functions quite differently from achievement
terms, precisely from the point of view of temporal structure.[20] He concludes that since seeing is not, at least not always, an achievement, it may turn out to be an activity
after all.

   There is no question that seeing can be an achievement in
our sense. Uses like *At that moment I saw him,* together
with the above-mentioned possibility of saying *I have seen
it* as soon as one is able to say *I see it,* show that much. I
shall refer to this "spotting" sense of seeing (which is somewhat analogous to the insight sense of *knowing,* or rather
understanding) as "seeing."
   Now, I think, "seeing" is not the only sense of seeing;

>   How long did you see the killer?
>   Oh, I am quite tall, I saw him all the time he was in
>   the courtroom. I was watching him.

suggests another possibility.

[18] Chap. v.   [19] Chap. vii.
[20] "Seeking, Scrutinizing and Seeing," *Mind,* LXIV (1955), 455–
478. On p. 472 he is induced to say things like "one must *throughout that length of time* be seeing it."

[113]

> Do you *still* see the plane?

points in the same direction. Furthermore,

> I spotted him crossing the street
> I spotted him running

can only be understood in the sense of

> I spotted him while he (or I) was crossing the street
> I spotted him while he (or I) was running.

On the other hand,

> I saw him crossing the street
> I saw him running

may also be taken to mean

> I saw him cross the street
> I saw him run.

Spot refuses this move:

> * I spotted him cross the street
> * I spotted him run.

Our time schemata explain this difference. Spotting (an achievement) connotes a unique and indivisible time instant. Now running or crossing the street are processes going on in time (the latter also takes time) and as such cannot be broken down into indivisible time instants: their very notion indicates a time stretch. Thus there is a logical difficulty in spotting somebody run or cross the street. One can spot somebody while he is running, or on the street, but *while* and *on* here indicate states, and states can be broken down into time instants. Then it is clear that seeing in

> I saw him while he was running (or crossing the street)

[114]

may mean merely "seeing," but seeing in

I saw him run (or cross the street)

must have a sense that admits a period of time: a process or a state.

But seeing cannot be a process. *What are you doing?* can never, in good English, be answered by *I am seeing* . . . . Thus notwithstanding the fact that one might see something for a long period, it does not mean that he "is seeing" that thing for any period, yet it remains true that he sees it at all moments during that period. In addition, *deliberately* or *carefully* fail to describe or misdescribe seeing, as no one can be accused of or held responsible for having seen something, though one can be accused of or held responsible for having looked at or watched something. Thus seeing is not an action which is "done" or "performed" at all. Finally the curious equivalence of *I see it* and *I can see it* or even *I saw him all the time* and *I could see him all the time* also confirms our claim that seeing is not a process but a state or achievement. Being able to see can hardly be conceived of as a process.

4.7.   At this point, however, a serious difficulty arises. After an eye operation the doctor might say that now the patient can see without suggesting that he sees through the bandage, much as he might say of a patient after an orthopedic operation that he can walk without implying that he is actually walking. Therefore—the objection might go—as the bodily state of being able to walk is not the same thing as walking, the bodily state of being able to see is not the same thing as seeing. Yet they are related the same way: the state of being able to walk is necessary for the activity of walking, and the state of being able to see is necessary for the activity of seeing. Furthermore, as we also suggested, we can say of a man who is sound asleep that he knows geography, or that he thinks that Jones is a rascal, or that he loves Lucy, but no one can say of somebody who is sound asleep that he sees something in any ordinary sense of *seeing*. One might say, however, that he can see, meaning that he is not blind. Thus to be able to see is a state like knowing but seeing is not.

This reasoning confuses two senses of *can*. There are people who can drink a gallon of wine in one draught. Suppose one of them has performed that remarkable feat a minute ago. Then it is quite unlikely that he can do it again now. Should we say then, at this moment, that he can, or rather that he cannot, drink a gallon of wine in one draught? He can and he cannot. Let us refer to the first *can* (in *he can*) as can_2, and to the second (in *he cannot*) as can_1. Of course, *he can_2* means that he $could_1$ if his stomach were empty. When his stomach is empty he both can_2 and can_1. Thus can_2 involves can_1 conditionally: he can_1 if certain conditions are fulfilled. Can_1 does not involve any further *can*-s: he can actually. Yet even *can_1 drink a gallon of wine* does not mean that he actually does drink or is drinking that amazing draught.

Now the doctor's *can* in *Now he can see*, spoken while the patient's eyes are still bandaged, is a can_2: if the bandage were removed and if his eyes were open (everything else, like light in the room, and so forth, remaining the same), then he $could_1$ see some things in the room; that is, he *would* see some things in the room. Thus the above-mentioned equivalence holds between *see* and *can_1 see*, that is, the lowest-level *can* that does not involve any further *can*-s conditionally. And this equivalence does not hold for activities: the other patient can_2 walk, though his legs are still tied to the bed; if he were released he could$_1$ walk, yet it may be he would not be walking.[21]

But my adversary might continue: "You obviously over-look a glaring difference. Walking is a voluntary action, while seeing is a spontaneous one. If you are not blind, if there is some light, and if you open your eyes, then you cannot help seeing something: the spontaneous activity of seeing starts. Digestion, you agree, is a process, yet the equivalence you speak about also holds there, because it also is a spontaneous activity. When I say that I can digest pork, I mean that if I had eaten pork, I could digest pork, that is, I would be digesting pork. If I have not eaten pork, I cannot digest pork. So there is a sense in which *can digest pork* and *is digesting pork* mean the same thing."

This objection is a shrewd one. It is quite true that no one can be running if he is not running, as nothing can be a cat if it is not a cat. But this *can* is a logical modality like *must* in

All cats must be cats.

In this sense, of course, *can be digesting* is the same as *di-gesting*. But our *can*, if you like, is a physical modality. It is silly to point at a pork chop and say

Now I cannot digest it, but when I have eaten it, I shall be able to digest it for a while, till I have digested it, and then I shall not be able to digest it any more.

But it is by no means foolish to say

[21] Now it becomes clear that, for instance, *He could$_1$ know the answer if he had read Kant* means that in that case he would know the answer, but *He could$_2$ know* . . . does not mean that in that case he would know the answer.

Now I cannot see the moon, but when the cloud goes away, I shall be able to see it.

4.8.   We can safely conclude then that seeing has a state sense too. Now, since there is no such process as seeing, yet there is an achievement of "seeing" (the "spotting" sense), the question arises whether "seeing" is related to seeing as catching dogs is related to the state of dogcatchers, or rather as "knowing" (the achievement) is related to knowing (the state). It is quite clear that the latter is the case:

At that moment I saw him (spotted him)

means that I did not see him before that moment. Thus "seeing" is an achievement initiating the generic state of seeing.

As will be recalled, there are scores of activities, accomplishments, and achievements involved in the notion of ruling or knowing that something is the case. Thus the problem remains: what activities, accomplishments, and achievements are connected in this way with the notion of seeing? Did I not know that Harvard is in Cambridge, I could not perform a great number of actions the way I do perform them. In an analogous way, if I do not see my hand, I cannot watch, scan, observe, or scrutinize it; I cannot gaze upon it, keep it in sight, focus my eyes on it, or follow it with my eyes; I cannot see that it is dirty, I cannot notice, or easily find out, tell, or describe what color it has or what it looks like at present; then also I cannot (in a sense) look at it and see it as an instrument or as an animal with five tentacles, and so on.

Of course, none of these actions have to be performed all at the same time, or one after the other, while we see an object. When I am writing, I see the pencil all the time, otherwise I could not write the way I do write. Nevertheless I do not watch, observe, or scrutinize it; I might not look at it at all; I might even not notice its color. In the same way, when I am walking up and down in my room, absorbed in thoughts, I do not pay any attention to the furniture around me, yet I see it most of the time; otherwise I would bounce against tables and chairs every so often. Think of the way we see our noses or the frame of our spectacles.

Notice that none of the actions I have enumerated are mysterious in the way that seeing is claimed to be mysterious. Any good dictionary can tell us what we mean by *watching, scrutinizing,* and so on, without even mentioning *seeing.*[22] On the other hand the meaning of *seeing* cannot be given, short of a mystery, without realizing its "state" as a state term, that is, without giving the kind of explanation I have tried to give. In much the same way, the meaning of *knowing* remains something ghostly till the kind of explanation is given that, for instance, we find in *The Concept of Mind;* or, for that matter, housekeeping would remain an abstruse activity did we not all know what sort of (by no means abstruse) actions housekeepers are supposed to perform.

4.9.   Before we take leave of *seeing,* I shall mention two borderline senses. If one tells us that he saw *Carmen* last night, he means that he saw all four acts of *Carmen.* Besides, he might say that it took three hours to see *Carmen.* Perhaps one might even answer the question *What are you doing?*

---

[22] For example, *The Concise Oxford Dictionary,* 4th ed., defines *watching* (relevant sense): keep eyes fixed on, keep under observation, follow observantly. And *scrutinizing:* look closely at, examine in detail.

by *I am seeing* Carmen *on TV*. Thus there is a queer accomplishment sense of *seeing*. There is another strained usage. A "seer" sees things, and now and then he actually is seeing ghosts or pink rats. Such strained or stretched employment should not worry us. It would be a very serious mistake if one tried to explain the stock uses of *seeing* on the basis of such employment.

Thus there is no one big mystery with regard to seeing, although little puzzles remain as to *observing, watching*, and so forth. One could point out, for example, that while they are activities, they sometimes have—and this is true more of *observing* than of *watching*—an accomplishment sense: it takes some time to observe the passage of Venus across the sun or to watch an ant carrying home a dead fly. There are obvious parallels between the concepts of seeing and hearing and those of watching and listening, and so on. Thus we could continue this kind of investigation, but without any specific problem it would become tedious and idle.

As a conclusion, I think, it is not too much to say that our categories, besides confirming established differences between processes and nonprocesses, may help us in clarifying the often overlooked and embarrassing differences within the class of nonprocesses. We have no reason to fear that seeing, for example, since it is not always an achievement, might turn out to be an activity after all, reviving thereby all the ghosts of epistemology. "What happens when we perceive, and what is it that makes it happen? That is the problem of perception." [23] A sailor on deck looking ahead remarks, "It is pitch dark, I don't see anything." After a while, "Now I see a star." We ask him,

[23] Boring, Langfeld, and Weld, *Foundations of Psychology*, p. 216.

"What has happened?" "The cloud's gone." "But what else happened?" "Nothing else." Of course many things happened in the world and in the sailor. But his seeing is not one of them.[24]

[24] I wish to express my gratitude to Professor Israel Scheffler for his helpful comments on the first draft of this chapter.

[5]

Facts and Events

5.1. In J. L. Austin's "Unfair to Facts" we find the following lines:

Phenomena, events, situations, states of affairs are commonly supposed to be genuinely-in-the-world, and even Strawson admits events are so. Yet surely of all of these we can say that they *are facts*. The collapse of the Germans is an event and is a fact—was an event and was a fact. Strawson, however, seems to suppose that anything of which we can say ". . . is a fact" is, automatically, *not* something in the world.[1]

I think Austin commits a mistake here, an important error in the sense that its correction leads one to a better understanding of a whole family of crucial concepts. As it is evident from the Austin-Strawson controversy, nothing less than the notion of truth and the relation of language and reality are tied up with this family. The same controversy reveals the extreme difficulty of the subject: Austin and Strawson would not continue disagreeing through "comments on comments, criticisms of criticisms" on obvious

[1] J. L. Austin, "Unfair to Facts," in *Philosophical Papers*, p. 104.

points.[2] I claim that the issues under discussion can be made reasonably clear by employing some recent results of linguistic theory which, at the time of the controversy, were not yet available to the protagonists. With these tools it will not be difficult to show that Austin's mistake is similar to the one committed in the following argument: "John's speech took place yesterday; John's speech was inconsistent; therefore, something inconsistent took place yesterday." Or, and this is closer: "John's death was painful; Mary denied John's death; therefore, Mary denied something painful." Sure enough, the collapse of the Germans was an event, and the collapse of the Germans is a fact. Yet it does not follow that some events are facts, or that some facts are events, nor that they must coexist in or out of this world. For one thing, those of us who followed the collapse of the Germans followed an event, but, surely, did not follow a fact. I do not imply that Austin was unaware of such differences: the very paper I quote displays his acute sense of language. What he lacks, however, is a framework into which the data can be fitted to form a pattern with clearly marked distinctions. Such a framework I want to propose.

Austin's mistake springs from the morphological identity of the subjects of sentences like

> The collapse of the Germans was an event
> The collapse of the Germans is a fact

or, to repeat,

> John's speech took place yesterday
> John's speech was inconsistent.

Yet, as is obvious in the second case, and as I hope to make obvious in the first, this morphologocial identity conceals

[2] *Ibid.*, p. 102.

[123]

important differences. These, however, cannot be located by the devices of traditional grammar, which will yield the same description for the parallel phrases in question. Of course, one can paraphrase the difference and say, for instance, that the delivery of John's speech took place yesterday, but the content of the speech was inconsistent. The trouble is that such paraphrases are usually offered *ad hoc*, following the speaker's linguistic intuition, which, in really difficult cases, may either fail or mislead. The question then arises whether it might be possible to systematize this procedure by finding standard and uniform sets of paraphrases for each opaque grammatical construction. It turns out that transformational grammar not only answers this need but goes beyond it both in technique and scope.

5.2.   If one asks the question, as Austin and Strawson do, what are facts, events, situations, states of affairs, and so on, the sensible way to start looking for an answer is to mention some particular instances that can be so qualified. The list thus obtained will show an interesting regularity. Most items on the list, if not all, will consist of a noun phrase containing a verb derivative, with or without its subject, object, or other complement. In technical terms, we will end up with a list of nominalized sentences. Austin's examples are no exceptions: *the collapse of the Germans*, and *the cat's having mange*. To these I have added *John's speech* and *John's death*. To indicate the wide variety of forms this construction can take, and the various ways in which it can occur, I give the following short list of sentences containing nominalizations:

> I know *that John died.*
> *His death* surprised me.
> *The selection of the jury* took up the afternoon.

I deny *ever having seen her.*
How he did it is a mystery.
John's being able to walk is the result of *an operation.*
It is better *to give* than *to receive.*
I like *John's cooking.*

These few examples are enough to show, first of all, the great frequency of such constructions in every sort of discourse. Accordingly, the grammar of nominalizations is a centrally important part of linguistic theory. The reason for this frequency of occurrence is easy to see: the device of nominalization transforms a sentence into a noun phrase, which can then be inserted into another sentence; it is a means of packing a sentence into a bundle that fits into other sentences. In these terms the distinction between the nominalized sentence (italicized in the examples) and the host, or "container," sentence becomes clear.[3]

5.3. When nominalizations are regarded in this way, the next questions to be asked follow naturally: what are the ways of transforming a sentence into a noun phrase and what, if any, are the restrictions governing the insertion of the nominalized sentence into the host sentence. We shall see that these two points are not unrelated; container sentences are selective hosts: open to a sentence nominalized in one way, they may refuse the same sentence when nominalized in another way. Even if we confine our attention to the forms relevant to our present purpose, we can easily find some illustrations. Consider the container

. . . surprised me.

---

[3] For a detailed discussion of nominalizations see R. B. Lees, *The Grammar of English Nominalizations;* Z. Vendler, *Adjectives and Nominalizations.*

[125]

What forms of nominalization can fill the subject position? The choice is wide:

> John's death surprised me.
> That he died surprised me.
> His having died surprised me.

Other containers are much more restrictive. Take

> . . . occurred at noon.

Here *John's death* is acceptable:

> John's death occurred at noon.

But not the other two:

> *That he died occurred at noon.
> *His having died occurred at noon.

Now take the two adjectival containers

> (1) . . . is unlikely
> (2) . . . is sloppy.

Then form two different nominalizations from the sentence

> John plays poker.

That is:

> (3) John's playing poker
> (4) John's playing of poker.

Clearly, (3) fits into (1) and (4) into (2) without any trouble:

> John's playing poker is unlikely.
> John's playing of poker is sloppy.

(2) will definitely reject (3):

> *John's playing poker is sloppy.

[126]

And even (1) will only reluctantly admit (4):

> ?John's playing of poker is unlikely.

One more example. The container

> I mentioned . . .

is more tolerant than the container

> I think . . .

The former admits both of the following:

> I mentioned that John died.
> I mentioned John's death.

The latter takes only the first form:

> I think that John died.
> *I think John's death.

5.4.　The considerations given in the previous section determine the strategy I shall follow. First of all I shall review the various forms that nominalized sentences (henceforth called "nominals") can take and shall try to find some ordering principle among them. Then I shall investigate the restrictions governing the compatibility of certain kinds of nominals with certain container contexts, hoping to end with a double result: classes of nominals corresponding to classes of containers. The tactical steps to be taken in this second task are marked out by the possible forms containers can have. Roughly speaking, a container pairs a nominal with a noun or with an adjective or with a verb. For example, each of the following sentences:

> It is a *fact* that John died
> His death was the *result* of an accident
> The collapse of the Germans was a gradual *process*

pairs a nominal with a noun; while each of the following:

> John's death was *painful*
> It is *unlikely* that he died

ascribes an adjective to a nominal. With verbs, there are two main possibilities: the nominal may be the subject of the verb, as in

> John's death *surprised* me
> His death *occurred* at noon
> Mary's arrival *caused* the confusion

or the nominal may be the object of the verb, as in

> I *denied* John's death
> I *heard* his singing.

At the end, the correctness of our conclusions will be subject to an indirect test: we shall see that the nouns, adjectives, and verbs that prove to be applicable to the same type of nominal fit one another as well. This result will not only reinforce our classifications, but will at the same time elucidate the concepts of fact, event, process, situation, and so on, and give us a hint concerning their ontological status.

5.5.   Before trying to fit nominals into containers, we must take a closer look at the nominals themselves. As I mentioned before, the essential ingredient of the relevant kinds of nominal is a verb derivative. This ordinarily consists of the verb root plus the suffix *-ing*. In addition, many verbs form second nominals by means of other suffixes: think of *death, refusal, explanation, move* (in this case the suffix is zero), and so on. Some verbs even have the luxury of possessing three or four nominals: *disposing, disposal, disposition*, for example, or *moving, move, movement, motion*. Fortunately, these variations do not materially affect our discussion. There is another form, however, which will have an independent role to play, and this is the familiar noun clause—for example, *that he arrives*.[4]

Next we have to consider other ingredients that may complete a nominal. First of all, the verb can take tenses, auxiliaries, and adverbs. The *that*-clause, obviously, is open to all of them: *that he arrived, that he is able to arrive, that he arrives unexpectedly*. The *-ing* form is equally liberal: *his having arrived, his being able to arrive, his arriving unexpectedly*. Other forms exclude these moves: *death* and *arrival* are immune to tenses or auxiliaries, and adverbs have to be changed into adjectives. This gives us the transformation exemplified by

> his arriving unexpectedly—his unexpected arrival
> his dying painfully   —his painful death.

The subject of the source sentence is left untouched in the *that*-clause, but has to be brought in by a genitive in other cases. Thus we have: *John's arrival, his death*, or, optionally,

---

[4] It is easy to show that even in contexts like

> We know that he arrived
> We know how he died

that and *how* belong to the verb object (which is a nominal) and not to the preceding verb. By forming the passive we get:

> That he arrived is known by us.
> How he died is known by us.

The situation is quite different in the case of, say,

> We found out the solution.

In this case *out* belongs to *found;* the passive is

> The solution is found out by us

and not

> * Out the solution is found by us.

the arrival of John. Confusion may arise from the fact that
the genitive also serves to include the object of a transitive
verb: *the execution of the criminal* or *the criminal's execution.* Hence the ambiguity in *the shooting of the soldiers.*
The ambiguity is resolved if both subject and object are
present: *His shooting of the soldiers* or *the shooting of the
soldiers by the prisoners.* Compare *the shooting of him, his
shooting,* and *the shooting of his.* In *the shooting of him*
he has to be the victim, in *the shooting of his* he has to be
the agent, and in *his shooting* he may be either. But this is
to digress. What is more important for us is the fact that
the *that*-clause cannot and the *-ing* form need not resort
to the genitive to keep the object; they can, so to say, keep
it straight: *that he sings the Marseillaise* and *his singing the
Marseillaise.* Notice that the object must be kept straight
whenever tenses, auxiliaries and adverbs are present. This,
of course, rules out constructions like

> *John's quickly cooking of the dinner
> *John's having cooked of the dinner
> *John's being able to cook of the dinner.

Negation, incidentally, shows the same restriction: while

> John's not revealing the secret

is all right,

> *John's not revealing of the secret

is not.

There is an important rule governing the omission of the
subject noun. If the object is kept straight, or if tenses,
auxiliaries, or adverbs are present, then the subjectless nominal cannot take articles or prenominal adjectives; if, on the
other hand, there are no tenses, auxiliaries or adverbs, and

if the object (if any) is in the genitive, then the subjectless nominal can take both. Thus while we have, for example, *singing the Marseillaise* or *singing beautifully*, we do not have **the singing the Marseillaise* or **the singing beautifully; the singing of the Marseillaise,* however, and *the beautiful singing* are again acceptable.

Not much ingenuity is needed to make sense of this welter of data. The salient fact seems to be the incompatibility of tenses, auxiliaries, and adverbs with articles, prenominal adjectives, and the objective genitive. Now since the former set of possibilities characterize verbs and the second nouns, we can safely conclude that the nominals under consideration fall into two categories, one in which the verb is still alive as a verb, and the other in which the verb is dead as a verb, having become a noun. The former is a case of arrested development; to use a previous analogy, the packaging process is incomplete; the verb still kicks within the nominalized sentence. In the latter case the packaging process reaches the verb itself and turns it into a noun. Harris uses another simile: he speaks of half-domesticated and fully domesticated nominalizations. I shall call the one with the live verb in it an "imperfect" nominal and the other, in which the verb acts like a noun, a "perfect" nominal.

5.6. The time has come to turn to our main task, that of determining the kinds of container sentence that are suited to receive these nominals. I suggested above that containers are selective: we shall find that the main principle of selection corresponds to the distinction just made between imperfect and perfect nominals. Unfortunately, this selectivity does not amount to mutual exclusiveness. Our work would be easy indeed if we could show a clear-cut distinction among containers in this respect. But then, probably, there

[131]

would be no errors to redress. As it is, instead of finding containers exclusively suited for imperfect or perfect nominals, as the case may be, what we find, if I may say so, are tight ones and loose ones—contexts, that is, of strict or lax hospitality. What I mean is this. We have loose containers that are able to receive the untidy package of imperfect nominals, but are at the same time tolerant enough to hold neat packages of perfect nominals as well, provided they are not too tightly packed. On the other hand we have narrow containers that are exclusively suited to perfect nominals. This result, in itself, would be significant enough. Yet this is not all. We shall see that when perfect nominals are offered in a loose container, the native speaker is ready to accept the corresponding imperfect nominal as a true paraphrase. To mention an example in advance, the sentence

The collapse of the Germans is unlikely

contains a perfect nominal in a loose context. The appropriate imperfect nominal in the same context

That the Germans will collapse is unlikely

is accepted as a genuine paraphrase of the same sentence. If, on the contrary, the same sequence is offered in a narrow container, as in

The collapse of the Germans was gradual

there is not even a possibility of paraphrasing it into

*That the Germans collapsed was gradual.

This fact leads to the important conclusion that in spite of their superficial tolerance, container sentences do discriminate quite sharply among nominals, and, in fact, may be more informative than the grammatical shape of the nominal itself. It is an interesting question, of course, what the reason is for the tolerance of loose contexts. I guess, but can only guess, that it is the greater versatility of perfect nominals; they are more fit to enter containers, since the process of nominalization is not arrested here. Yet one cannot overdo things. If the nominal is too tightly bundled, the loose container tends to reject it or, at least, there are some rumbling noises. For example, while

> The singing of the Marseillaise is unlikely

may pass,

> The beautiful singing of the Marseillaise is unlikely

is at least questionable and

> John's beautiful singing of the Marseillaise is unlikely

sounds horrible. Why is this so? The answer seems to be that since perfect nominals shed tenses and auxiliaries, too much of the relevant information is lost in the packaging process. Indeed, the last sentence can be reduced to a number of alternatives. For example,

> It is unlikely that John sang . . .
> will sing . . .
> can sing . . .

What we see here is an interesting conflict between two tendencies: preservation of information content and simplification of form. There are good reasons to think that our language is somewhat unsettled, or even that it is undergoing a change, in this matter. This uncertainty, however, affects the surface rather than the substance.

[133]

5.7.   I shall begin by examining loose containers, that is to say, containers primarily suited for imperfect nominals. Therefore I take the following battery of phrases: [5]

> that John sings
> John's singing the Marseillaise
> John's having sung
> John's being able to sing
> John's singing well.

Then, following the plan outlined at the beginning of Section 5.4., I ask the question: what are the adjectives that fit them? Clearly not words like *yellow, round, fast, easy*, or *clever*. That is to say, not adjectives of the lower ranks, in terms of a classification I shall develop later.[6] Thus we are left with such adjectives of the highest ranks as *possible, useful, necessary, likely, probable, certain, true*, with their opposites, and the omnipresent *good*. I do not claim that all of them go with all imperfect nominals. There are manifold restrictions here, but for our present enquiry I can omit these refinements. So instead of giving an elaborate table of possible co-occurrences, I shall resort, here and in the sequel, to the stratagem of selecting a few paradigm examples. In this case I pick *unlikely, probable*, and *certain*. It is easy to see that they go with all relevant forms:

> That John sings is unlikely.
> It is unlikely that he sings.
> John's having sung the Marseillaise is unlikely.
> His being able to sing well is unlikely.

---

[5] The notion of a "battery" of transformations is due to H. Hiż. See his "Congrammaticality, Batteries of Transformations, and Grammatical Categories," *Proceedings of the Symposia in Applied Mathematics*, American Mathematical Society, 12 (1960), 43–50.

[6] See Chapter 7.

The same holds for *probable* and *certain*. It is interesting to realize that most, but not all, of these adjectives are unsuited for nouns that are not nominals. There are no probable dogs, certain trees, and unlikely cigars, or, if there are—well, then we have a little explaining to do.

Now we turn to verbs that take imperfect nominals for subjects. From a great variety I select *surprise* and *cause* as paradigms. Indeed we have the following:

> That John sang the Marseillaise surprised me
> His being able to sing well surprised me

and also

> John's singing the Marseillaise caused the riot
> His having sung the Marseillaise caused the commotion.

Here, again, most of these verbs are reserved for nominal subjects. (*Cause* even has the peculiarity of requiring a nominal in object position as well; tables and horses are not caused by anything. But this and related points I shall take up in the next chapter.)

A great number of verbs either require or tolerate imperfect nominals for object. *Mention, deny,* and *remember* may serve as paradigms:

> He denied that John sang the Marseillaise.
> I mentioned his being able to sing.
> I remember his having sung.

Finally, some containers pair nominals with nouns. Here our paradigms will be *fact* and *result:* [7]

[7] Interestingly enough, these nouns, as well as the container nouns to be given for perfect nominals, i.e., *event, process,* and *action,* are themselves nominals—of Latin ancestry.

It is a fact that John sang the Marseillaise.
His being able to sing well is a fact.

From these we even can form compound nominals like:

the fact that John sang the Marseillaise
the fact of his being able to sing well

which, once more, can enter container contexts. As to
result:

John's being able to sing is the result of long training.
That he sang the Marseillaise was the result of drinking five martinis.

This last example shows, incidentally, that the things denoted by such nominals can not only be results but can also
have results: we mentioned the result of John's drinking
five martinis.

The phrase I just used—"we mentioned the result"—
reminds us of the indirect proof I promised a while ago.
This proof consists in showing that container elements—
nouns, verbs, and adjectives—that fit one class of nominals
fit each other as well. Indeed, results and facts, to stick to
our paradigms, can be mentioned, denied, or remembered.
Similarly, both facts and results may surprise us. We also
can talk of facts or results causing other things. As to adjectives, it is obvious that all three paradigms cheerfully take
result: many results are unlikely, probable or certain, not
to mention possible, useful or even true results. *Fact* is more
selective, but this is understandable in view of the strong
achievement-sense of this word: remember that *true fact*
is redundant and *false fact* is a contradiction. But this is a
different story. At any rate, the indirect proof seems to
work, and it will gain in impressiveness as we shall be able
to compare and contrast the container family belonging to

imperfect nominals with that belonging to perfect nominals. The collection of this latter one is the next item on our agenda.

5.8.   A battery of perfect nominals can be given by the following selection:

> the singing of the Marseillaise
> the beautiful singing
> John's singing of the Marseillaise.

As we look for adjectives and prenominal or postnominal verbs that apply to these forms, we must not be disturbed by the fact that a good many of the container elements associated with imperfect nominals are also applicable here. I explained above that by the use of paraphrastic transforms we can clear up the muddle. What we have to look for here are narrow containers applicable to perfect nominals only.

Most of the adjectives meeting this requirement will belong to the class I shall A_3's,[8] of which *slow*, *fast*, *sudden*, *gradual*, and *prolonged* are typical instances. It is clear that their role is quite different from the role of adjectives characterizing imperfect nominals. Compare:

> John's singing is possible.
> John's singing is slow.

The first has the transform

> It is possible that he sings

but the second does not have

> *It is slow that he sings.

The second sentence, on the other hand, turns into

---

[8] See Chapter 7.

John sings slowly

while the first cannot be forced into

*John sings possibly.

The best we can do is this:

John, possibly, sings.

If the difference is still not clear enough, think of the possibility of hearing slow singing and the impossibility of hearing possible singing. But this is to anticipate. Note, incidentally, that not all perfect nominals can take all A_3's. There are some co-occurrence restrictions here, which, however, do not change the grammatical situation. The collapse of the Germans can be slow, fast, sudden, or gradual; the singing of a song, however, can be slow or fast, perhaps even sudden, but hardly gradual.

There are a few nouns that can be predicated of perfect nominals; for example, *event, process,* and *action:*

> The collapse of the Germans was a gradual process.
> The murder of Caesar was a bloody event.
> Johns' kicking of the cat was a deliberate action.

The class of container verbs is the most characteristic here. Among the prenominal ones we find *see, watch, hear, feel, observe,* and so on. For instance:

> I heard the singing of the Marseillaise.
> I felt the trembling of the earth.
> I watched the execution of the criminal.
> I observed the passage of Venus.

Postnominal verbs are not less revealing. Here we have *occur, take place, begin, last, end,* and so forth:

The running of the race took place at Belmont.

The uprising began in May, lasted for two months, and ended in July.

John's singing of the Marseillaise occurred after midnight.

Here I add that certain temporal prepositions fit perfect nominals, but not the other kind. *Before, after, since,* and *until* are such. While

Everything was quiet until his singing of the Marseillaise

The trouble started after the singing

pass all right,

* Everything was quiet until his singing the Marseillaise

* The trouble started after his singing the Marseillaise

do not.

5.9. I claimed above that while container contexts suited for imperfect nominals are fairly tolerant towards perfect nominals, the reverse is certainly not the case. I do not have to belabor this point; a few examples will suffice:

* John's singing the Marseillaise was slow.

* The Germans' having collapsed was a gradual process.

* I heard his having sung the Marseillaise.

* John's kicking the cat occurred at noon.

As for loose or tolerant contexts, the device of paraphrastic transforms is needed to clarify the confusion they create. Consider the ambiguity in

[139]

John's singing of the Marseillaise surprised me.

Since *surprise* is a loose container verb, the sentence can be taken in the sense of

That he sang the Marseillaise surprised me.

But it need not be taken in this way. It may be that it was something about his singing that surprised me; his pleasant voice perhaps. So we might say:

That he did it in a pleasant voice surprised me.

What is important here is that the verb *surprise* pushes us, as it were, toward an imperfect nominal. Sometimes we have to recover the nominal. Take:

John surprised me.
John caused the trouble.

In both cases we sense an invitation to complete the sentences: he surprised me or caused the trouble by doing something. (Not, incidentally, by the doing of something.) In the case of, say,

John ate an apple

one does not feel the push; the sentence is complete. One more example: if we say

The abominable snowman is a fact.

what we mean is this: the existence of that monster (that it exists) is a fact. On the other hand, the sentence

The abominable snowman lives in caves

is complete. It is not its existence (life or presence) that lives in caves. These are cases of suppressed nominals. To complete the picture, I want to say a few words about disguised nominals. There are certain nouns that are not verb derivatives, yet behave like nominalized verbs; that is, they can enter container contexts without suggesting suppressed nominals. Fires and blizzards, unlike tables, crystals, or cows, can occur, begin, and end, can be sudden or prolonged, can be watched and observed—they are, in a word, events and not objects.

5.10. We come now to our second indirect proof: container elements that fit perfect nominals are suited to each other as well. It is events, processes, and actions, and not facts or results, that occur, take place, begin, last, and end. The former, and not the latter, can be watched, heard, followed, and observed; they can be sudden gradual, violent, or prolonged. The converse, due to the looseness of the containers, is not so obvious on the surface. Yet, even if we speak of mentioning, though not of denying, events, processes, or actions, even if we call them unlikely or probable, even if we allow them to cause things or surprise us, we at once feel the push toward saying that it is really something *about* them—their occurrence or some quality—that we refer to.

I add a nice point that confirms our main result.[9] If a sentence is not nominalized at all, it still shows an affinity toward contexts that are suited to imperfect nominals, but not to those fitted for the other sort. The nominal *John's death* may figure in both kinds of context: John's death may surprise us, and John's death may be slow. If we do not nominalize, we still can have

John died, which surprised me

but not

* John died, which was slow.

[9] This point I owe to H. Hiż.

To summarize, we have defined, on purely syntactical grounds, two families of nominals, imperfect and perfect. We found that container contexts clearly discriminate among them—to such an extent, in fact, that in dubious cases the quality of the container sentence decides the affiliation of the nominal in question.

5.11. It is time to return to Austin's example: *the collapse of the Germans*. This phrase, in itself, presents a dubious case, in spite of having the form of a perfect nominal. Nobody would object to the sentences:

> The collapse of the Germans is a fact.
> The collapse of the Germans was an event.

But we know that the contexts in which the nominal, *the collapse of the Germans*, occurs in these sentences determine an entirely different set of paraphrases and possible co-occurrences for each; in other words, the senses in which the nominal is taken in these two cases are categorically different. As it by no means follows that since the collapse was a gradual or bloody event, the fact of that collapse has to be gradual or bloody, and as it by no means follows that since the fact of that collapse has been denied or contradicted, any event has to be denied or contradicted, so it is equally absurd to conclude that since the collapse of the Germans was an event that took place in the world, any fact has to take place or simply be in the world. Austin's syllogism has four terms.

5.12. If catching Austin napping on one occasion were the only result we could show for our prolonged labors, we could justly be accused of shooting pigeons with elephant guns, or, shall I say, batteries. No, our final quarry is of far nobler breed. Hence a metaphysical cauda to the linguistic tale.

What is in the world? More specifically, are there only objects in the world, or also events, actions, and processes, or perhaps even facts? The reason for this threefold distinction is obvious by now: it simply mirrors the subdivision of noun phrases into object nouns and the two kinds of nominal we have discussed. I do not think that the question just posed is philosophical nonsense. It cannot be, since I am going to answer it in what I hope is a sensible way.

We have talked enough, directly and indirectly, about facts and events. To be able to answer the question, we will have to add some very obvious points about objects, and discuss a few perhaps less obvious points about the concept of the world, particularly with respect to the phrase *being in the world*.

As for the concept of an object, I once more follow the procedure of asking what sorts of adjectives and verbs are available in talking about objects. In doing this, I have to to be selective: I choose those that are relevant to the present topic. And, since we are aware of the linguistic background, I shall avail myself of the comforts of the material mode. So I draw attention to the fact that objects have sizes and shapes, one can touch them, look at them, and see them from various angles and distances. Moreover we can push and pull them, cut them or tear them apart. This is possible because they are located at a certain place, they are somewhere. And they can change place by moving, rolling, or walking, by rising or falling. They can, in addition, contain other objects as boxes do cigars. All this and many other features can be summarized by repeating the trivial truth: objects are in space. Are they in time too? The answer is not easy. Objects do not occur, begin, or end. They are in a place, but they do not take place at a certain time. They do not even last except with respect to wear. To say that a tree began twenty years ago, lasted for ten years, and then ended is to talk philosophical nonsense. Yet, for sure, they may exist for a length of time. But then it is their existence, or life, that lasts that long. Prepositions tell the same story. Although we might speak of times before Socrates or after Christ, what we mean is something like before or after their birth or public life. This is enough to show that the relation of objects (or persons) to time is different from that of events, actions, or processes; it is an indirect relation.

Events and their kin are primarily temporal entities. A quick glance at the relevant verb class, together with a consideration of adjectives like *fast, slow, sudden, prolonged,* and *gradual,* prepositions like *before, after,* and *since,* are enough to convince us. Are they in space? Not directly. The collapse of the Germans is not located, nor can it be found anywhere. Yet it makes sense to say that it took place both in the *Vaterland* and in occupied Europe. Yet to continue by saying that the collapse of the Germans was 2,000 miles long would be absurd. Yes, the collapse may have occurred all along a 2,000-mile front, but this precisely shows the indirect relation that events have to space.

Now facts (and their kin, like results) are not in space and time at all. They are not located, cannot move, split, or spread, and they do not occur, take place, or last in any sense. Nor can they be vast or fast. Sentences like

> For many years it was a fact that Africa was dominated by European powers.

is just a journalistic transform of

> It is a fact that for many years Africa was dominated by European powers.

[144]

5.13. Finally, what about the world? Is it something like an object, or something like a process, or something like a fact? Well, what can we say of the world? Surely, it is large and wide. We are *in* it and some things in it are closer to us than others; we speak of *this part* of the world. True, the world cannot move and is not somewhere, but this should not disturb us in view of the relativity of these concepts. It seems, then, that the world is very much like an object; more exactly, the idea of the world is the limiting idea of the totality of all objects. Objects are parts of the world, somewhat as organs are parts of an organism. Then, surely, objects are in the world in a very straightforward sense.

Yet the coin has another side. It is possible to speak of the beginning or the end of the world. We even say that in spite of John's death the world goes on as before. If, therefore, the world is also a process, then other processes may be in it as parts: much the same way as the writing of this chapter is a part of my life. But even this process aspect of the world aside, all processes, actions, and events take place *in* the world in the indirect sense I mentioned above.

But how can facts possibly be in the world? When they cannot even be in more familiar receptacles like rooms or continents? Certainly facts are *about* things in the world, but this *about* is not the *about* of *she is working about the house all day*. It is the *about* of *talking about something*. I do not find any justification for the claim that facts are in the world.

This brings us back to the correspondence theory, Austin's demonstrative and descriptive conventions, and the maxim, "A statement is true if it fits the facts." [10] If the correspondence theory requires a relation between empir-

---

[10] "Truth," *Philosophical Papers*, pp. 85–101.

ical statements and observable entities in the world, then facts are not qualified for this latter role. Objects and processes might be, but then I do not know how to formulate the theory. Fortunately, this is not my task in this chapter. But what about the principle, "A statement is true if it fits or corresponds to the facts"? Does it not suggest a relation between statements and the world? It cannot and it does not. First of all, notice that we do not say, in the singular, that a true statement fits a fact. We say, in the plural, that a true statement fits the facts. This can only mean that it is consistent with and is in harmony with the facts known or knowable that are relevant to a given case. It is like saying that a theory fits the data. And, since we know that facts can be stated and denied, it is not surprising to find that they can be consistent with, entail or be entailed by, statements, results, other facts, and so on. Needless to add that consistency and entailment are not relations affecting observable things in the world. The maxim "True statements fit the facts" has nothing to do with the correspondence theory of truth.

[6]

Effects, Results,
and Consequences[1]

6.1.   It is well-known in theory, though often not sufficiently realized in practice, that some key terms of philosophical discourse lead a double life. We understand and
use them in our daily intercourse, and we claim we understand them as they occur in the writings of philosophers,
in spite of the fact that the conditions of their use in these
two cases are contextually or even grammatically different.
This of course means that we are really dealing with more

---

[1] This topic was originally suggested to me by the late J. L.
Austin in 1955. The present chapter is a somewhat enlarged com-
bination of two papers that appeared in *Analytical Philosophy* (ed.
R. J. Butler) "Effects, Results and Consequences" (pp. 1–15) and
"Reactions and Retractions" (pp. 25–31). In trying to improve the
originals I was greatly helped by the comments of Professors S.
Bromberger, W. H. Dray (published in the same volume), and
Ruth Barcan Marcus. I was also impressed by the excellent dis-
cussion of the original papers by Professor J. M. Shorter entitled
"Causality and a Method of Analysis" in *Analytical Philosophy*,
second series (ed. R. J. Butler).

than one concept: our ability to understand such a term in its natural habitat does not guarantee, per se, that we are able to understand it when it is transplanted into the gardens of philosophy. Accordingly, we have to learn the new concept (or concepts) from the philosophical texts themselves.

Acclimatizations of this sort are not peculiar to the language of philosophy. Most terms of science are also borrowed from ordinary discourse. The notions of mass, force, energy, and so on, all show this cleavage, while that of, say, an electron is wholly indigenous to physics. What is peculiar to philosophy, however, is the role such transplanted words play. In science, terms are part of the entire conceptual apparatus with which, to quote Kant, we "approach nature in order to be taught by it." [2] But what does the philosopher approach with his revalued terms? By what does he expect to be taught?

The philosopher can give either of two accounts—one modest, one ambitious. The former may run as follows: "All I do is to propose a new way of looking at the world. In order to share my view, among other things you have to master the concepts I suggest; if you look at things in these terms, you will see. . . ." Far be it from me to quarrel with such philosophers. If I did, not only they but the whole tribe of poets, artists, and prophets would line up against me—a prospect I could not face. My complaint is against the ambitious philosopher. His line runs something like: "My aim is logical analysis. If you follow me I shall solve your philosophical perplexities by analyzing and clarifying the notions involved, and I shall show. . . ." Now I ask: What notions is he going to analyze? The original notions that gave rise to the problems, or the notions he creates in the very course of his discussion? If the former, all is well;

[2] Kant, *Critique of Pure Reason* B xiii (N. K. Smith trans., p. 20).

if the latter, all he says is likely to be trivial; if, finally, he does the second and claims he does the first, all he says is likely to be wrong.

6.2.   Cause and effect are perhaps the most beloved couple in the history of philosophy. And for the same reason, they are among the best examples of concepts that have the double life I mentioned above. Moreover, in this case, not unlike the cases of such other favorites as the mind and the soul, the cultivated line threatens to invade the legitimate domain of its natural ancestry. Educated people are but little surprised to hear, for instance, that the shoe is the effect of the shoemaker, parents are causes of their children, God is a cause and the world is his effect; they are ready to believe that collisions of billiard balls, criminal tendencies, rising unemployment, the creation of symphonies, and so on, are all effects that clamor for their causes, namely for forces, substandard housing, economic depression, or moods of Beethoven. After all, according to Locke

That which produces any simple or complex idea, we denote by the general name *cause;* and *that which is produced, effect.* Thus finding that in that substance which we call 'wax' fluidity . . . is constantly produced by the application of a certain degree of heat, we call the simple idea of heat, in relation to fluidity in wax, the cause of it, and fluidity the effect. So also finding that the substance, wood, . . . by the application of fire is turned into another substance called ashes, . . . we consider fire, in relation to ashes, as cause, and the ashes, as effect.[3]

Again, Hume himself assures us that "all causes are of the same kind" [4] and that " 'tis possible for all objects to become

[3] Locke, *An Essay Concerning Human Understanding,* II. 26.
[4] Hume, *A Treatise of Human Nature,* I. iii. 14.

causes or effects to each other." [5] Following these principles, he writes of "all the long chain of causes and effects
which connect any past event with any volume of history"; [6] and he asserts that "whether a person openly abuses
me, or slyly intimates his contempt, in neither case do I
immediately perceive his sentiment or opinion; and 'tis only
by signs, that is, by its effects, I become sensible of it." [7]
Similarly, Kant views as a cause "a ball which impresses a
hollow as it lies on a stuffed cushion," and he claims that "a
glass (filled with water) is the cause of the rising of the
water above its horizontal surface," and that "the stove, as
cause, is simultaneous with its effect, the heat of the room." [8]

These quotations should be enough to indicate the reality
of the problem. Philosophers have created a notion of cause
and effect, or, rather, each philosopher has created his own
notion of cause and effect and has then proceeded to analyze
that notion and reach conclusions about it. And, if he was
consistent, he got out of his investigations exactly what he
put into them.

The reason for this curious procedure is not far to seek.
In ordinary language we have a fairly large group of words
that are felt to belong to the same family. *Cause, reason,
source, origin, maker,* and so on, form one branch of the
family; *effect, result, consequence, work, product, creation,
offspring, upshot,* and so forth, the other. Philosophers, trying to exploit this intuition, began to call all members of the
first group causes, and all members of the second effects. In
doing so, however, it was easy to overshoot the mark and
to mistake the unity of a synechdoche for the unity of a
genus. They forgot, in other words, that mere family re-
semblance is not a sufficient foundation for a common
genus. Consequently, unless it is shown that conclusions

[5] *Ibid.,* I. iii. 15.   [6] *Ibid.,* I. iii. 13.   [7] *Ibid.,* I. iii. 13.
[8] *Op. cit.,* B 248 ff. (Smith, pp. 227 ff.).

arrived at on the basis of these self-made genera indeed apply to the range of the original concepts, such conclusions will remain irrelevant with respect to the genuine problems connected with the same concepts.

It would require a book, one worth undertaking, to cover this whole field. In this chapter I shall limit myself to a few examples, mainly taken from the "effect" list, to show the dimensions and the magnitude of the logical differences we encounter there, differences which have been largely ignored throughout the long history of the problem of causal relations.

6.3.   The procedure I am going to follow, at least at the beginning, cannot be a systematic one, since one does not know, in advance, what aspects of the total logical picture are relevant. Thus discovery and resolution must go hand in hand: categories will emerge as a result of differences, and differences will be found by applying the categories.

With such caution, I start with the privileged member of the group, effects. Indeed, what are they? Consider the following hypothetical account.

The effects of the atomic explosion could be felt within a radius of a hundred miles. Sensitive instruments, like seismographs, could measure and register them thousands of miles away. The immediate effects, heat, radiation, air pressure, earthquakes, and tidal waves, reached in themselves a large area; and if one adds the more remote effects, such as radioactive fallout, the poisoning of the atmosphere and the sea, one can imagine the disastrous effects such an explosion would have on a densely populated region.

This, I think, is a fairly typical context involving the term *effect*. If so, it can be used to discover the main aspects of the concept.

First, let us pay some attention to the things that are called effects: heat, radiation, pressure, earthquake, tidal wave, fallout, and the poisoning of the atmosphere. From a linguistic point of view the most obvious feature of this list is the preponderance of nominalizations. This impression can be strengthened by realizing that genuine nouns can hardly fill the bill. No one would call a crystal, a plant, an animal, or a piece of furniture an effect of anything. True, we may speak of watches, purses, or jewelry as personal effects, but this peculiar and rather restricted use of the word is obviously irrelevant to the discussion of the "causal" sense of *effect*—the sense, that is, in which we speak of the effects of explosions, actions, restrictions, and the like. The consideration of word co-occurrences points to the same direction. The effects of an explosion are not yellow or pink, square or oval, hard or soft, they cannot be found on mountain tops or gathered and transported into a museum. In view of what we said toward the end of the previous chapter these facts clearly indicate that effects are not objects. What are they?

The theory of nominalizations we gave in the same chapter, incomplete as it is, may prove helpful once again. The question to be asked, therefore, is whether the noun phrases to which the word *effect* is properly adjoined satisfy the transformational and co-occurrence criteria of imperfect nominals or rather those of perfect nominals. If a clear pattern emerges, we will know what kind of thing effects are —whether they are like events (processes) or like facts.

A careful rereading of the quoted text will convince us that the nominals involved have to be perfect nominals; effects are events or processes in the world and not facts. That the earth shook violently is not the effect of the explosion: it is the violent shaking of the earth, itself, which is the effect. This, and not the former, can reach a large area; this can be felt, registered, and measured. That the earth shook is not violent or dangerous, but the effect of the explosion, the shaking of the earth, is violent and dangerous. We do not say

> The earth's having shaken was an effect of the explosion

but we do say

> The shaking of the earth was an effect of the explosion.

The crew of the Nautilus is protected against the effects of nuclear fission: they are protected against radiation, which can penetrate thick walls and harm the organism, and not against the *fact* of radiation, which cannot penetrate anything and is quite harmless to the body. The characteristic phrase *has an effect on something* reinforces the conclusion that effects are not products or facts. The effect *on* something is a change or process, which that thing undergoes.

The arguments contained in the previous paragraph could be expanded and offered in a more rigorous fashion. By a systematic application and extension of the method sketched in the previous chapter it could be demonstrated that the phrase . . . *is an effect of* (*something*) is a container sentence suited to receive perfect nominals in its blank; in other words, that the word *effect* applies to the same general category of entities to which the words *event* or *process* can be properly applied. The difference is the following: while these last words are, as it were, single containers, *effect* is a double container. It turns out that the *something* in . . . *is an effect of something* is but a dummy for another perfect nominal. If an event or process is described as an effect, then it is attributed to something, and that something will be another event denoted by another perfect nominal. We were discussing the effects of an atomic explosion, an explosion that took place somewhere, that may have been sudden or violent, that could be watched, and so forth. The "paradigm" containers for perfect nominals turn up again. Imperfect nominals will not do:

> *The earthquake was the effect of the bomb's having exploded.
> ?That the bomb exploded had an effect on the atmosphere.

Hence the possibility of effect chains. Radiation is an effect of the atomic explosion, but radiation itself may have various effects on living tissues, say malignant growth, the terrible effects of which, in turn, may spread throughout the organism.

One may object here that sometimes effects are attributed not only to other events, but also to objects or people. We often say things like

> Hitler had a hypnotic effect on his audience.
> The moon has an effect on the surface of the oceans.

My answer is that in these cases I can predict the existence of other sentences, like

> Hitler's speeches had a hypnotic effect on his audience.
> The moon's attraction has an effect on the surface of the oceans.

These sentences do contain nominals to which the effects are really ascribed, and they are clearly recognized by the fluent speaker as less elliptical, more explicit, versions of the former sentences. This is not the case with sentences like

> Hitler had a brown coat.
> The moon has no vegetation.

Here we cannot insert a nominal into the blanks in

> Hitler's . . . had a brown coat.
> The moon's . . . has no vegetation.

Thus we realize that the counterexamples are based on what we called above (in 5.9) "suppressed" nominals.

By way of summary, we may say that effects are not facts or physical objects, but events or processes which are due to other events or processes in the world.

6.4. Our outline of what effects are will show a still sharper contour as we presently proceed to compare results with effects. First, a rough contrast: it does not make sense to say that one feels or measures results; they cannot reach large areas or penetrate thick walls; they cannot be prevented, yet no organism needs to be protected against them; they are not sudden or prolonged, violent or mild, cooling or sedative; nothing, finally, has a result on anything else. Results, accordingly, are not effects, because, as we are going to show in detail, they are not events or processes at all.

We have to begin with a distinction that is easier to feel than to express. It is obvious that when we speak of the results of tests, experiments, games, elections, calculations, and so forth, we are using the term in a different sense from the one that is implied in talking about the results of earthquakes, floods, wars, revolutions, accidents, or what not. An experiment, for instance, is a procedure one pursues with the aim of obtaining a specific piece of information, and the piece of information thus acquired is the result, in this qualified sense, of the experiment. In another sense, of course, the experiment may have many other results. As a result of that experiment a theory may be refuted, new methods of production may be developed, the scientist performing it may become famous, he may be promoted, or as a result of that same experiment he may have contracted epidermic cancer. In a similar way tests, games, elections, and the like, may have all sorts of results besides the results in the qualified sense. These latter may be copied, posted, published, filed, and so on, which is not customary with respect to results of earthquakes and wars, or with respect to the various results experiments, games, or elections may have in addition to their qualified results. In reproducing qualified results we usually resort to more or less direct quotation:

> The results are as follows: ". . ."

or

> As a result of the experiment we know (or we can say) that . . .

Unqualified results are commonly reproduced more indirectly:

> As a result of the experiment new methods of production have been developed

or

> The introduction of the new methods was the result of that experiment.

Since I am interested in relations that are traditionally called causal, I shall not be concerned with results in the qualified sense, but focus my attention on the more general, unqualified sense of *result* although, as it will appear, the use of the same word here is more than accidental. Following my procedure, I begin with another hypothetical context:

As a result of the H-bomb explosion in the Pacific, a whole atoll has disappeared, leaving a gaping hole in the ocean floor. Fishermen scores of miles away contracted radiation sickness and some of them died. Moreover, the whole region became contaminated for weeks. If these are the results of just one such explosion, what would be the results of an all-out nuclear war? Contamination of the whole atmosphere, poisoning of food, genetic changes, and perhaps the extinction of the human race. Such horrible results surely cannot be aimed at by any of the potential belligerents.

As we see, nominals turn up again. Thus *result*, no less than *effect*, is a container noun. Unlike *effect*, however, *result* is a tolerant container (see 5.6–9), which means, as we remember, that it is primarily suited to receive imperfect nominals—in other words, nominals denoting factlike entities. This can be shown by several arguments along the lines laid down in the previous chapter.

In the first place, all these nominals can be transformed into noun clauses: the results of a nuclear war would be that the atmosphere would be contaminated, that genetic changes would occur, that the human race might die out, and so on. For that matter, the results of the explosion in the Pacific could be given a similar formulation. One result was that an atoll disappeared, another that some fishermen died, and so forth. Moreover, nominals thus used can take tenses and modal auxiliaries. One might say that an atoll's having disappeared was a result of the explosion, as one might say that our being able to destroy ourselves is a sad result of advanced technology. There are negative results too: not preventing a nuclear war may be the result of bad will or indolence.

The second argument can be derived from the kind of adjective appropriate to the word *result*. Effects, as we saw, can be strong or weak, violent or mild, sudden or prolonged. Results, on the other hand, do not take these adjectives. They are usually qualified as being fortunate or unfortunate, expected or unexpected, sad, disastrous, or horrible. It is easy to see that only this second group enters the construction.

It is *A* that (something is the case).

The first group, the one appropriate to *effect* fails to do so:

*It is violent (sudden, etc.) that (something is the case).

As there are no violent or sudden facts, so there are no violent or sudden results.

Finally, results, not unlike facts, can be mentioned, stated, expressed, known, believed or disbelieved, denied or contradicted. Moreover, interestingly enough, just as there are no false facts, in some sense there are no false results either. Even in the qualified sense, false or incorrect results are hardly results at all. *Result*, from this point of view, belongs with such achievement nouns as *reason*, *cause*, *motive*, and *explanation*.

There is an important use of the word *result*, however, which at first glance seems to contradict our conclusion. One certainly can point at the ruins of Coventry and say

Look at the results of the war.

Again, we often encounter sentences like

Petroleum is a result of organic corruption.

[158]

Being stubborn, I once more resort to the stratagem I employed to explain away Hitler's effect on his audience. Are there no suppressed nominals here, which could be made explicit? I make a very modest claim: I suggest that the existence or origin of those ruins is a result of the war, and that the formation of petroleum is the result of organic corruption. The point is that I *can* make these or similar claims. In other contexts I could not. Those ruins are in Coventry, but the existence of those ruins is not in Coventry. Some lamps burn petroleum, but they do not burn the origin or the existence of petroleum. A thing is not the same as its origin, formation, presence, or existence. Yet, in some contexts, we mention the former instead of the latter:

Flies are impossible in this climate

instead of

The existence of flies is impossible in this climate

and

Dogs are not permitted in this house

instead of

The presence of dogs is not permitted in this house.

Thus the counterinstances can be dismissed once we recognize the metonymy on which they are based.

Above we mentioned the possibility of effect chains. Are there result chains? Undoubtedly. The success of foreign competition is a result of the high American prices, which are a result of the high wages, which are a result of the power of labor unions, and so on. Results are facts and they are due to other facts. The death of those fishermen was the result of the fact that they had not been informed of the impending explosion.

Now we see the real contrast between effects and results. Speaking the effect language we are talking about the dependence of events and processes in the world; using the result language we talk about the relation of facts. To say that the tidal wave is an effect of the earthquake is different from saying that the tidal wave is a result of the earthquake. The tidal wave as an effect—that is, as a process—is strong at the center but weakens with distance; it lasts for days and reaches vast areas where it can be felt, observed, or measured. The tidal wave as a result—that is, the fact of the tidal wave—is neither weak nor strong, it does not last, does not spread, and cannot be watched. On the other hand, unlike the former, it can be asserted and denied, believed and disbelieved, remembered or forgotten. The difference between them is not merely generic, it is categorical.

6.5.   As to consequences, it is easy to see that they are akin to results rather than to effects. Without running through the whole battery of tests, I shall just mention a couple of decisive points. Consequences, like results and unlike effects, can be formulated in noun clauses; they can be stated, told, believed or disbelieved; they are probable or improbable, expected or unexpected, but never sudden, prolonged, violent, mild, or penetrating. Far-reaching effects reach far in space: far-reaching consequences do not. Consequences, therefore, are also facts, and not objects, events, or processes.

This is sufficient to discriminate between effects and consequences. The distinction, however, between results and consequences is far less sharp, and is not easy to draw.

The first thing we have to realize is that the difference is most obvious in connection with human actions. We rarely speak of the consequences of explosions, earthquakes, or cosmic radiation. Next, we may note two peculiarities. It makes sense to say that we aim at or achieve certain results, while it is nonsense to talk about aiming at or achieving certain consequences. The lucky man, as the joke goes, gets results; the unlucky one gets consequences. The latter, as it were, arise unasked for; the agent can be warned of the consequences of his action, he may try to avoid them, and, sometimes, he has to face them. These things are hardly true of results. Again, while we may distinguish between intended and unintended results, this distinction is out of place with respect to consequences. There are no intended consequences, and therefore it would be redundant to say that the consequences of an action were unintended. It seems to me, therefore, that states of affairs due to human action can be viewed in two ways. Inasmuch as they are considered in connection with the actual or possible intention of the agent we are inclined to speak of them as results. If, however, they are considered in abstraction from such intention, we prefer to call them consequences. The vagueness of this formulation corresponds to the blurred boundary line between these two notions: what makes unintended results results rather than consequences? Perhaps what we have in mind is this: had the agent known that this (favorable) thing would come out of his action, he would have intended it. This line of thought seems to imply that all unintended results are unforeseen, a conclusion that appears to be quite plausible.

Effects, as we saw, turned out to be events or processes, while results and consequences proved to be facts. The question naturally arises: are there no objects that are due to other things, and if there are, what do we call them?

This question leads us to consider some other members of the effect group of terms: *product, work, creation,* and so on. Now I see no reason why one should stop here; one might continue: *offspring, child, fruit, secretion,* and so on. The only ordering principle of this series is that of decreasing generality. The common feature of the terms of the series is that they are predicated of physical objects or persons which are attributed directly or indirectly to other physical objects or persons.

The shoe is the shoemaker's product, *The Thinker* is Rodin's work, and a gown may be Dior's creation. There are some subtle differences within the group itself, of which I mention just two. One can say that the shoe is the product of the shoemaker's labor, but not that *The Thinker* is the work of Rodin's labor. This seems to indicate that while products are attributed to the agent's action and only indirectly to the agent, works are directly attributed to the agent himself. Anybody can answer the question: out of what did the shoemaker produce (or make) the shoe? But how should one answer the question: out of what did Dior create that gown? Out of silk, or out of his head? Think of God creating rather than producing or making the world *ex nihilo.*

It seems to me that the remaining members of the effect family—upshot, issue, outcome, and so on—do not offer anything new or really instructive: their significant logical features could be located by means of the tests already used, and described in terms of the categories thus far given.

6.6. Having thus drawn a somewhat detailed picture of the effect group, we can open some further perspectives by examining the relation of its members with the privileged member of the other group, that is to say, with causes. Do effects have causes? Or is it rather results that are due to causes? Or is it products?

At this point we reach the most surprising conclusion of this whole chapter. I have good reasons to think that no effect is the effect of any cause. The principle, "All effects have causes" is by no means analytic: if it is taken to mean that any effect is the effect of some cause or other, then the principle is false and, if I may say so, analytically false; if it merely means that a thing that can be called the effect of something may *also* be caused by something or other, then the principle may be true.

I am going to demonstrate that if it true that X is the effect of Y, then Y cannot be the cause of X. Half of the task has already been accomplished. On the basis of our discussion of effects we know that effects are events or processes, which are attributed to other events or processes *in rerum natura;* effect chains are homogeneous. The other half of the argument will consist in proving that causes are not events or processes, but rather factlike entities, as results and consequences appeared to be. At the same time it will transpire that the things that are caused are events or processes and not factlike entities. This asymmetry can be understood in terms of the linguistic background. The word *cause*, like *effect* or *result*, is a double container: *X is the effect of Y, X is the result of Y,* and *X is the cause of Y,* each calls for a pair of nominals to replace the variables. Now while *effect* and *result* require nominals of the same kind for X and Y, that is, perfect nominals for *effect* and imperfect ones for *result, cause* requires an imperfect one for X and a perfect one for Y; *cause* is a "mixed" double container; it accounts for an event by means of a fact.

Before going any further I wish to pause long enough to

[163]

reflect upon the syntactical versatility of the word *cause*. It is either a verb or a noun. Except for a peripheral case, however, this duplicity has no influence on the co-occurrence requirements of the word. The sentences

> The explosion caused the tidal wave
> The explosion caused the building to collapse (or the collapse of the building).

can be paraphrased by the transforms

> The explosion was the cause of the tidal wave
> The explosion was the cause of the collapse of the building.

Unfortunately, such a move will fail with respect to a more complex construction. The sentence

> John caused the butler to ring the bell

does not have an *X is the cause of Y* equivalent. The result of our attempt:

> ?John was the cause of the butler's ringing of the bell

is a grammatical monster and even if we accept it, it will not do as a paraphrase of the original. In view of this, the fact that here a genuine noun and not a nominal, *John*, is the subject of *cause* is far less disturbing than it would be were this reduction a success.

For, needless to say, I want to claim that neither causes, nor things caused can be objects or persons. In the matrix *X is the cause of Y*, the variables do not stand for simple nouns but for nominals. Counterexamples like

> John caused the disturbance

can be made harmless by pointing to the possibility of inserting a nominal and producing the fuller form

John's doing something caused the disturbance

following the precedents given above in similar situations.[9] This conclusion, of course, rules out persons or objects from the ranks of causes, and products, works, and so forth, from the class of things that are caused. Tables and chairs are not caused by anything.

6.7. It is easy to show that the word *cause* is a loose container with respect to X in the paraphrastic frames X *causes* Y and X *is the cause of* Y. The existence of the following sentences puts this beyond doubt:

John's having arrived caused the commotion.
John's being able to come caused our surprise.
John's hitting the bartender caused the fight.
The cause of the fight was that John hit the bartender.

I continue by pointing out that there are negative causes, as there are negative facts and negative results. We can say

[9] As Dray pointed out, there is a fine difference in meaning between, say,

John caused the disturbance by walking out

and

John's walking out caused the disturbance.

The former seems to attribute responsibility, the latter does not. I think this is due to a difference in emphasis. *I enjoy reading Milton* has a different emphasis from *I enjoy Milton* (try to add . . . *but not reciting him* and . . . *but not Dante*, respectively) even though in both cases it is the reading of the works of Milton which is enjoyed. Transforms (including deletions) of the same sentence may emphasize diverse elements without altering the original grammatical structure.

that John's not seeing the red light caused the crash, or that the signalman's failure to pull the switch caused the accident, and we may add that the signalman's failure to pull the switch was the result of his hangover. Now it is obvious that John's not seeing the red light or the signalman's failure to do something cannot be construed as events or processes. Accordingly they cannot be things that have effects either: John's not seeing the red light caused the crash, yet the crash is not the effect of his not seeing the red light. In the same way, his hitting the bartender may have caused the fight, yet the fight was by no means the effect of his hitting that poor man.

Finally, in examining adjectives that the word *cause* can take we see at once that they agree with those appropriate to results, and differ from those we found suited to effects. Causes are never strong or weak, violent or mild, sudden or prolonged, dangerous or harmless; but they may be likely or unlikely, probable or improbable, proximate or remote (not proximate or remote in a physical, but rather in a logical sense). Similarly, causes, like results and unlike effects, can be stated, told, learned, remembered, or forgotten, but not felt, watched, observed, or measured.

6.8.   Having thus shown that causes are factlike entities I proceed to examine the status of things that are caused. The possibility of causal chains seems to offer an easy short cut. One might argue as follows: effect chains were possible because both variables in the frame X *is the effect of* Y stood for perfect nominals, result chains were possible because both variables in the frame X *is the result of* Y represented imperfect nominals; consequently, if there are causal chains, then we can be sure that both variables in the frame X *causes* Y stand for imperfect nominals, that is, noun phrases denoting factlike entities.

Well, there are causal chains. Here is one:

During our famous seventeen consecutive days of below-freezing temperatures, the moisture in the ground under the pavement turned to ice, which caused the ground to swell, which caused the pavement to rise, which caused the asphalt to crack.[10]

In all three cases the pronoun *which* is the subject of *cause*, thus it must replace an imperfect nominal. Since, moreover, *which* here introduces appositive relative clauses, it must be apposited to an identical noun phrase preceding it in each case. But that noun phrase is the verb object of *cause* in two instances. *Ergo,* the same noun phrase can occur in either place in the *X causes Y* frame. Hence it follows that it is factlike entities that can be caused, just as it is factlike entities that are the causes.

How great then is our disappointment to realize that this beautiful argument must be fallacious and that our easy shortcut has landed us in a mire. For, as it turns out, the verb object of *cause* must be a perfect nominal: *X causes Y* is a strict container with respect to *Y*. It receives perfect nominals without resistance:

> The explosion caused the collapse of the building.
> The rising of the temperature was caused by the sunshine.
> The deviation of the missile was caused by faulty guidance.

As we experiment with imperfect nominals, the results are more or less questionable:

> ?The explosion caused the building's having collapsed.

[10] Adapted from *The New Yorker*, March 25, 1961, p. 29.

> ?(The fact) that the temperature rose was caused by the sunshine.
>
> ?The missile's having deviated was caused by faulty guidance.

Again, nominals containing negatives or modals fail to qualify. We recall that John's not seeing the red light caused the crash and that his being able to come caused our surprise. Such things, however, cannot be caused:

> * His not seeing the red light was caused by dense fog.
>
> * His being able to come was caused by clever planning.

The trouble is with the word *cause:* if we substitute *was due to* for *was caused by* the sentences pass all right. Indeed, *X is due to Y* connects two imperfect nominals; facts may be due to other facts. On the other hand, clearly, facts may be causes, but they cannot be caused.

One more illustration. The sentence

> He is ill

has the imperfect nominal forms

> that he is ill
> his being ill

and the perfect one

> his illness.

Just remember that it is his illness and not his being ill that can occur, begin, and last for some time. Now, I think, it is his illness, and not his being ill, that can be caused by something or other. Yet his being ill may cause many things: one might say, for instance, that the chairman's being ill caused the delay in the proceedings. The fact that we can also say that his illness caused the delay should not disturb us. After all, the point is precisely that X *causes* Y is a loose container for X and a narrow one for Y.

6.9.   Where, then, is the fallacy in the short-cut argument given above? The answer is that we were too hasty in assuming that the appositive relative pronoun must replace a noun phrase which is identical, at least in category, with the noun phrase to which it is apposited. We took it for granted, for instance, that since what caused the pavement to rise was the fact that the ground had swollen, we had to interpret the phrase

. . . caused the ground to swell

in the sense of

. . . caused the fact that the ground has swollen.

The relative pronoun, however, is far more tolerant. Remember, from 5.10, the example

John died, which surprised me

in which *which* is apposited to *John died* as if it were a nominal. Remember, too, footnote 10 from Chapter II. We remarked there that in the sentence

I bought a house, which has two stories

which really stands for *the house I bought* and not just for *a house*. In view of these examples the short-cut argument need not force us to abandon the conclusion arrived at on the basis of more reliable data. I feel, nevertheless, that our results should not be interpreted too rigorously. Fine points of grammar are open to exceptions or even to change. But, then, we have no alternative to tracing these features and

[169]

following them where they lead, delicate and fragile as they are.

6.10.   What shall we say, finally, of the principle, "All effects have causes"? Effects, which are processes, are effects of other processes: effect chains are homogeneous. Causes, which are facts, cause processes: causal chains are heterogeneous. Now, do effects have causes? The answer seems to be this: the kind of thing that can be an effect of something may be attributed to a cause, but it is not the effect of that cause. In other words, the proposition "Some effects have causes" may be contingently true. Do *all* effects have causes? The question can be put in the following form: is it true that for any relevant choice of X and Y, given the sentence Y *is the effect of* X, there will be a corresponding form X' *causes* Y (where X' is the imperfect nominal derived from the same matrix sentence as X)? The problem would require a detailed study, into which I cannot enter now. The reverse, for one thing, is certainly false. There are choices of X' for which the transformation from X' *causes* Y to Y *is the effect of* X breaks down. Given, for instance,

His not seeing the red light caused the crash

we would get the unacceptable

   * The crash was the effect of his not seeing the red light.

In general, effects, results, or consequences have no specific counterparts. Nor do causes, on the other hand, have specific counterparts. As to the dependence of one object or person upon another object or person we have a much richer terminology ranging from product to child on the

[170]

one side and from maker to parent on the other. Some of these are obviously coordinated. And, as there is no common genus to which effects, results, consequences, products, and so forth belong, so there is no common genus to which causes, makers, parents, and so on belong. To say that the former are all effects and the latter all causes, or that their relation is a causal relation, is like saying that objects, events, and facts are all things, and what they share is being. Such locutions, of course, fail to tell us anything about what objects, events, or facts are, and by the same token, they are quite useless in helping us to understand the concept of effects, results, consequences, or, for that matter, causes in the true sense. The work remains to be done.

[7]

The Grammar of Goodness[1]

7.1. "If I am asked 'What is good?' my answer is that good is good, and that is the end of the matter." [2] In spite of this famous disclaimer, Moore still has a few things to say about good. For him it turns out to be a simple quality, like yellow, although, unlike yellow, a nonnatural one. What is the sense of this last claim?

Can we imagine "good" as existing *by itself* in time, and not merely as a property of some natural object? For myself, I cannot so imagine it, whereas with the greater number of properties of objects—those which I call the natural properties— their existence does seem to me to be independent of the existence of those objects. They are, in fact, rather parts of which the object is made up than mere predicates which attach to it. If they were all taken away, no object would be left, not even a bare substance; for they are in themselves substantial and give to the object all the substance that it has. But this is not so with good.[3]

[1] This is a somewhat revised version of a paper of the same title that appeared in the *Philosophical Review*, LXXII (1963), 446–465.
[2] G. E. Moore, *Principia Ethica*, p. 6.   [3] *Ibid.*, p. 41.

This quality, in other words, is more remote from the thing than other qualities: while these latter ones, as it were, make up the thing itself, goodness is attached to the thing already complete.

In this chapter I do not want to take up the metaphysical view concerning objects and their qualities that Moore presupposes in his account. What I am interested in are the reasons behind Moore's intuition: why did he feel and, for that matter, why do we feel, that goodness is more remote from the thing than color, shape, or other qualities? What I hope to show is this: the adjective *good* is more remote from the grammatical subject than adjectives like *yellow* or *round*. As we realize that ascribing the predicate *good* to a subject is a more complex and less immediate move than, say, ascribing the predicate *yellow*, we also realize the grounds for the feeling or intuition concerning the intimate connection between a thing and its color (or some other "natural" quality) and the less intimate tie between the thing and its goodness (or some other "nonnatural" quality). We shall encounter, once more, an instance of metaphysical intuition mirroring a feature of grammar.

7.2.   In order to define the connection between the adjective *good* and the subject to which it is ascribed, I have to raise the general question: what are the ways in which adjectives can be tied to subjects? As we shall see, there are many such ways; moreover, it will turn out that for each adjective only some of these are open. This fact affords us a principle of classification for adjectives in general and a method of discriminating between the various kinds of use a single adjective may have. The results of a detailed examination of one particular adjective, *good*, may serve as an illustration of the philosophical relevance of a linguistic study of this kind which, if carried out in full generality, might amount to a complete treatment of qualities.

Recently Paul Ziff has subjected *good* to a detailed and penetrating semantic analysis.[4] In doing so he has also discussed some points concerning the grammar of the word. I particularly refer to his observations about the relatively high "rank" of this adjective.[5] This means that it is likely to appear at the beginning of an unbroken string of adjectives in prenominal position: *good heavy red table* rather than *heavy good red table* or *red heavy good table*, and so on. The reason for this high rank, he suggests, is the relatively great privilege of occurrence of *good*. Take the sentences:

(1) This is a good table.
(2) I had a good sleep.
(3) It is good that it is raining.

These are perfectly acceptable. Yet the substitution of *heavy* for *good* will spoil the sentencehood of (3), and the substitution of *red* for *good* ruins both (2) and (3). These and similar examples show, therefore, that *good* enjoys a greater privilege of occurrence than *heavy*, and *heavy* greater than *red*. Accordingly, the order of rank will be *good heavy red* and no other. Ziff himself is clearly aware of the shortcomings of this principle. In face of several counter-examples he concludes that "some principle other than simple privilege of occurrence must be at work here. Semantically speaking, it appears to be one having something to do with natural kinds but I can provide no satisfactory syntactic characterization." [6]

---

[4] P. Ziff, *Semantic Analysis*, Chap. vi.   [5] *Ibid.*, pp. 203 ff.
[6] *Ibid.*, pp. 205–206.

[174]

To Ziff's counterexamples I would like to add one more. It is clear that *comfortable* outranks *red: comfortable red chair* and not *red comfortable chair*. Yet it is equally clear that *red* has a far greater privilege of occurrence than *comfortable*. Roughly speaking, there are many times more nouns that can be qualified by the former than by the latter; on the basis of merely counting heads, *red* is the winner. But then I ask the question: why is it that it makes sense to say that a chair is comfortable, but not that an apple is comfortable? What is a comfortable chair? One that is comfortable to sit on. Now is a red chair red to sit on? We at once realize that *red* does not admit the context: *It is red to. . . . Comfortable*, on the other hand, always connotes a verbal structure. A ride can be comfortable and so can be the coach in which one rides. Then what would be a comfortable apple? *This apple is comfortable to* do what? What emerges here is that while redness is attributed to a thing directly, being comfortable is attributed to it only with respect to an appropriate action involving that thing. Here we have the first example of adjectives being tied to their subjects in different manner. And, I add, the rank of an adjective depends upon the quality of this tie; *red*, for instance, comes closer to the noun than *comfortable* because it joins the noun in a more direct and immediate manner.

Ziff realizes that the higher rank of *good* sets it apart from adjectives denoting colors, shapes, or "natural kinds." Moore feels that, while these adjectives correspond to natural qualities, *good* stands for a nonnatural one. Moore's claim is based on intuition; Ziff tries to find grammatical criteria but, I think, mistakes a symptom for the cause. What do we do, what linguistic paths do we have to follow,

[175]

when we say that something is good? The importance of this question will justify, I hope, the discussion of some technical details.

7.3. Above, in 2.8, I suggested that the source of the prenominal adjective construction is the restrictive relative clause. A noun phrase like

> red hat

is to be derived from

> hat that is red.

This move conforms to the transformation

> (I) AN—N wh. . . is A

This, no doubt, represents the transformational origin of a great many adjectival noun phrases. It would be a mistake, however, to think that all *AN* phrases conform to this pattern.[7] Examples like

> beautiful dancer
> utter fool
> nuclear scientist

are sufficient to caution us. No fool is utter and a nuclear scientist is not a scientist that is nuclear. And what about the beautiful dancer? The phrase may mean two things: either that the dancer is beautiful or that she (or he) dances beautifully. Now an adequate transformational analysis must reflect this difference. Consequently, while (I) may be behind the first sense of the phrase, the second calls for another source.

To locate this source, I propose to analyze the sentences:

[7] P. T. Geach, in "Good and Evil," *Analysis*, 17 (1956), 33–42, arrives at a similar conclusion from logical rather than linguistic considerations.

> She is a beautiful girl.
> She is a beautiful dancer.

The derivation of the first is unequivocal:

> She is a beautiful girl.—She is a girl who is beautiful.

The second admits two derivations:

> She is a beautiful dancer.—She is a dancer who is beautiful.
> She is a beautiful dancer.—She is a dancer who dances beautifully.

The important point is that in this last case the adjective is not tied to the subject by the copula, but by another verb (to dance). This verb, of course, is recoverable from the noun (dancer) attributed to the same subject. The adjective (beautiful), therefore, is not ascribed to the subject (she) directly, but only with respect to a noun or, rather, with respect to a verb recoverable from that noun. This suggests the derivation:

$$(\text{IIIa}) \quad AN_V-N \ wh. \ . \ . \ VD_A{}^8$$

Not all adjectives fit into both patterns. Compare:

> She is a blonde and beautiful dancer.
> She is a fast and beautiful dancer.
> *She is a blonde and fast dancer.

The situation is as follows: *blonde* conforms to (I) but not to (IIIa); thus it pulls *beautiful* into the former. *Fast* con-

---

[8] N_V here represents an "agent"-nominalization formed out of a verb; e.g., *dancer, swimmer, cook, judge*. D_A stands for an adverb derived from an adjective; e.g., *beautifully, slowly, fast*, and so on. The numbers assigned to this and the following transformations reflect a theoretical order, which is somewhat different from the order of this exposition.

forms to (IIIa) but not to (I), so it forces *beautiful* into (IIIa) as well. Consequently, *beautiful* ceases to be ambiguous in the first two cases. In the third case the opposing forces clash head on, so that the resulting sentence becomes deviant. The full analysis shows the trouble clearly:

> *She is a blonde and fast dancer.—She is a dancer who *is* blonde and who *dances* fast.

Blonde is tied to the subject by the copula, *fast* by the verb *to dance*. Therefore the conjunction breaks down. Such a combination test is a powerful tool in deciding upon the identity or difference of transformational history.

We just said that *fast* cannot conform to (I) and that it conforms to (IIIa). If so, the question arises, what to do with phrases like *fast horse*. Here no verb is recoverable from the word *horse*. Yet we understand what the phrase means: a fast horse is one that runs fast. We have to say, therefore, that the co-occurrence of *fast* and *horse* must define a verb (or verb class) that connects the adverb *fast* with the noun *horse*, similar to the way in which the verb *to dance* connects *fast* (or *beautiful*) with *dancer*. This explains why we fail to understand phrases like *fast apple* or *fast chair;* these co-occurrences do not yield a connecting verb. *Round apple* or *red chair*, on the other hand, do not need any connecting link beyond the copula; therefore we understand them at once. The verb class involved may be small or large. In the case of *fast horse* we have hardly more than one such appropriate verb. But take *weak king*. He rules or governs weakly. Finally, in cases like *careful mother* or *good man*, the class becomes larger and larger. Yet, we feel, even these combinations must connote appropriate verb classes. We understand what they mean, but hardly, without further information, what *careful brother* or *good planet* means. The inclination to say, for instance, that a careful mother *mothers* carefully is significant: we resort to the clumsy verb to represent the class. For these reasons we can indicate the transformational source of these adjectival phrases by an extension and generalization of (IIIa):

$$\text{(III)} \quad AN\!-\!N \text{ wh. . . } [V]D_A{}^9$$

(IIIa), then, is a special case of (III): the verb is not merely connoted by the noun; it is morphologically recoverable from the noun.

As we saw, not all adjectives can enter both (I) and (III). *Blonde*, for instance, is restricted to (I), *fast* to (III), while *beautiful* can take either. This fact, together with further results, affords us a classification of adjectives. Accordingly, I shall affix $_1$ to those entering (I), $_3$ to hose entering (III), and so on: red_1, $blonde_1$, $fast_3$, $careful_3$, $beautiful_{13}$, or, in terms of variables A_1, A_2, A_3, A_{13}, and so forth.

Certain nouns appear to be partial to A_3's. There is some oddity in phrases like *blond king, tall mother, fat father*, and others. These nouns explicitly denote certain functions (appropriate verb class), so when they are used with an adjective, we expect one qualifying them with respect to that function. Indeed, why should one say *tall mother*, when *tall woman* is available? Such nouns can be recognized by another peculiarity, too. Given an indeterminate sentence like

> He is good
> She is careful

in which the noun providing the appropriate verb class is missing, we can supply this deficiency by the following construction:

---

9 [V] stands for the "appropriate" verb class.

He is good as a king.

She is careful as a mother.

This device is restricted to explicitly functional nouns. Although we understand phrases like "fast horse" or "good car," we cannot say:

*This (animal) is fast as a horse.

*This (vehicle) is good as a car.

This means that these nouns are only implicitly functional. Accordingly, phrases like "fat horse" or "red car" are not subject to the oddity mentioned above.

7.4. This last point leads to another important class of adjectives. Consider the phrases:

small elephant

short python

big flea.

Now it is obvious that although all elephants are animals, a small elephant is not a small animal; no more is a big flea a big insect, nor, for that matter, is a small factory a small building. A yellow factory, on the other hand, is indeed a yellow building, and an angry elephant is an angry animal. The peculiar feature of these "measuring" adjectives is brought out by the usual paraphrases:

small for an elephant

short for a python

big for a flea.

The form of another paraphrase would be: *small as elephants go*. Both versions, of course, presuppose a standard size, length, weight, or some other dimension corresponding to each specific noun. Adjectives, therefore, attributing ex-

[180]

cesses or defects with respect to that standard, form the contrasts

> big—little
> long—short
> thick—thin
> heavy—light

and so on. That these contrasts, as it were, belong to one another can be shown by two other tests. Questions formed in terms of one can be answered by using the other:

> How big is it? It is small.
> How long is it? It is short.

Moreover, the denial of one leads to the assertion of the other. An elephant that is not small is big (or average); a flea that is not big is small (or average).

Notice that these features do not apply to A_1's. One does not say that a yellow house is yellow for a house; one cannot ask how yellow it is, and answer that it is blue; finally, one cannot argue that since it is not yellow it is blue or average. As for A_3's, there seems to be some similarity: many A_3's form contrasts: *fast—slow, strong—weak, careful—careless, good—bad,* and others. This, however, should not mislead us. A_3's, by their very nature, must have adverbial derivatives. Measuring adjectives, on the other hand, usually do not (*big, small, tall, low*) or, if they do, the derivative has a remote, often metaphorical, connection with the source (*shortly, narrowly, lightly*). This fact, by itself, rules out (III) as possible source. Again, while A_3's presuppose appropriate verb classes, measuring adjectives do not. What peculiar verb class is required for the understanding of *big flea?*

What, then, is the transformational origin of noun phrases

involving measuring adjectives? The following comparison will help us:

> This is a yellow horse.—This *is* a horse which *is* yellow.
>
> This is a fast horse. —This *is* a horse which *runs* fast.
>
> This is a small horse.—This *is* a horse which *is* small *for* a horse

In the first case *horse* and *yellow*, as it were, stand on the same footing: tied to the subject by the copula. This is the most immediate link. The other two cases display a more remote connection. *Fast*, as we saw, is tied to the subject by a verb (class) determined by a logically prior predication of a noun. *Small*, though tied to the subject by the copula, applies to it only with respect to a noun predicated of it again with logical priority. On this basis I suggest the following schema for AN phrases containing measuring adjectives (henceforth called A_2's):

> (II) AN—N wh. . . is A for an N

7.5. We just said that an A_1 is tied to the subject in the same way as a noun predicate, that is, by the copula. Then it is not surprising that A_1's turn out to be nounlike in other respects too. First of all, some of them occur as nouns as well:

> He is a German.
>
> That yellow is lovely.

In addition, for many of them we can ask in terms of a noun:

> What *kind* of animal is it? Crustaceous.
>
> What is its *color?* Red.
>
> What is its *shape?* Round.

[182]

Indeed, some A_1's denote kinds, species, genera, nationalities, religions, and so on, while others name colors and shapes. There is an interesting difference between the two groups: individual things belong to species, genera, and so forth, but not to colors or shapes. In Aristotelian terms, the former are secondary substances, the latter are not. Yet even these seem to have some sort of existence of their own. One can say, for instance, either that an apple is red or that its color is red, either that it is round or that its shape is round. Now to say that the apple is red is to attribute a color to the apple, but to say that its color is red is not to attribute a color to that color; that color is red by identity: red is a color. Using Aristotle's words again: redness is not only predicated of but also is present in the primary substance.[10] I think these are the facts behind Moore's remarks about "natural" qualities: "They are . . . rather parts of which the object is made up than mere predicates which attach to it . . . they are in themselves substantial." Finally, there is a grammatical difference between color and shape words, too: one can say that one likes red, but not that one likes oval; names of colors are more nounlike than names of shapes. Many more details would be necessary to establish the conclusion I propose here: among the subclasses of A_1's those denoting kinds are the most nounlike, followed by names of colors, shapes, and finally, by other A_1's like *gay*, *sad*, *pretty*, *ugly*, and so on. These last are more or less contrastive, and thus form a bridge toward A_2's. A_2's are still less nounlike than color or shape words. Red is a color, round is a shape, but long is not a length, low is not a height, heavy is not a weight (except in boxing and the like), and small is not a size (except in clothing and the like). A house has a certain color, and that color may be red: it also has a certain height, but that height is not high or low.

[10] Aristotle, *Categories*, II–V.

Red is the name of a color; *height* and not *high* is the name of a dimension. Yet to ask how long a thing is is to ask for its length, to ask how high it is to ask for its height, and so on. For A_2's only vestiges of nounlikeness remain.

Now I claim that the natural order of these adjectives (the order of their rank in Ziff's sense) is a function of their connection with the subject, which, as I tried to indicate, is related to their nounlikeness. Adjectives with closer ties—that is, more nounlike ones—come closer to the noun. Some examples:

> large tawny carnivorous quadruped
> thick retangular green Oriental carpet
> tall round wooden structure

and, to repeat Ziff's example,

> good heavy red chair.

Later on we shall be able to complete this picture. In any case, Ziff's surmise that the principles determining the rank of an adjective have something to do with natural kinds has been confirmed.[11]

7.6. The derivations thus far covered are by no means sufficient to account for all adjectival constructions. Compare:

[11] It is interesting to realize that (I) is not the only way in which A_1's can be attached to nouns. While, for instance, a red lamp is a lamp that is red (I), an infrared lamp is not a lamp that is infrared: an infrared lamp is one that gives infrared light. This suggests the transformation:

(Ia) AN—N[V]A[N]

(where [V] and [N] stand for appropriate verb or noun classes) which covers a multitude of cases like *nuclear scientist, yellow fever, Wagnerian soprano,* and so on.

good cook
good meal.

A good cook, according to (III), is a person who cooks
well. Now what about *good meal?* Obviously, this phrase,
too, requires an appropriate verb (class); this will be *to eat:*
a good meal is good to eat. The difference between the two
derivations is this. In the first case *cook* is the subject of the
appropriate verb, in the second case *meal* is the object of
that verb: the cook cooks, but the meal is eaten. In both
cases the verb can be nominalized; thus we get:

good cook—good at cooking
good meal—good to eat
—good for eating.

We can say, then, that while *good* is attached to *cook* with
respect to a complete verb phrase, *good* is attached to *meal*
with respect to a verb phrase minus its object (or other
noun complement). Similar analysis is called for in cases
like

comfortable chair—comfortable to sit on
easy problem —easy to solve.

This corresponds to the schema:

(IV) AN—N wh. . . is A to V—

Incidentally, the subject of the original sentences may be
brought in by a preposition:

It is a good meal for you to eat.
It is an easy problem for me to solve.

Of course, here too the verb (class) depends upon the
noun. We remarked above that while there is no trouble
in understanding what a good mother or a weak king is,

[185]

we do not understand what a careful brother or a good planet might be: the co-occurrences *careful—brother* and *good—planet* do not define verb classes. Now the same thing holds with respect to (IV): *good meal, easy problem, difficult language, comfortable chair,* are understandable because we find appropriate verbs. *Good planet* and *easy tree,* however, remain mysterious even from this angle. Yet they become clear as soon as the speaker supplies the relevant verb: *good planet to observe, easy tree to fell.* Notice, of course, that it is not the planet that does the observing and not the tree that does the felling; that is, these are cases of (IV) and not of (III). In certain instances we can supply a verb either for (III) or for (IV):

She is good

can be completed as:

She is good at dancing (III).
She is good to dance with (IV).

At this point it might be useful to summarize our findings concerning the adjectival constructions represented by (I)–(IV). (I) exhibits an immediate connection between the subject and the adjective. In (II), (III), and (IV) the connection is not immediate. (II) presupposes an intervening noun, (III) and (IV) require appropriate verbs; in (III) the subject remains in that position even with respect to these verbs, while in (IV) it is regarded as their object.

7.7. The next group to be considered ascribes the adjective to the subject with respect to a whole sentence sharing the same subject. This class (A_5's) comprises adjectives like *clever, stupid, reasonable, kind, nice, thoughtful, considerate,* and *good* again. The following characteristic forms reveal the nature of the connection just mentioned:

John is stupid to take that job.
It is stupid of John to take that job.
John is good to help his brother.
It is good of John to help his brother.

The difference from (IV) is obvious. It is John who is stupid and it is John who takes the job: both sentences have the same subject. In (IV), however, the subject qualified by the adjective becomes the object of the sentence containing the appropriate verb; think of *good soup* which presupposes the soup eaten and not eating. The difference from (III) is a more delicate matter. Compare *slow*$_3$ and *considerate*$_5$. The superficial difference is easy to draw. John may cook slowly, but it is not slow of him to cook; *vice versa*, it may be considerate of him to cook, yet this does not mean that he cooks considerately. We can locate a deeper difference if we recall what we learnt in Chapter 5. *Slow*, clearly, turns out to be a container adjective and an intolerant one at that. It is predicable of perfect nominals without trouble:

His cooking of the dinner was slow.
The singing of the song was slow.

Imperfect nominals are rejected:

*His cooking dinner was slow.
*His having cooked was slow.

A few parallel tests would demonstrate that all A_3's are such strict containers. A_5's, however, are not:

It is considerate of John to cook dinner.
It was considerate of John to have cooked dinner.

As we see, the verb *to cook* may keep its object straight, and can take tenses. The nominal, with respect to which *considerate* is ascribed to *John*, is an imperfect nominal. In common-sense terms, what *slow* describes is the doing of the thing; what *considerate* describes is the thing done.

A_3's, A_4's and A_5's show a curious ambivalence. If John cooks slowly, we can say that he is slow in his cooking or that his cooking is slow. In a similar way, we may either say that he is considerate to cook dinner or that to cook dinner is considerate of him. *Slow* or *considerate*, therefore, can either be ascribed to a nominal or to the subject of the nominal. An A_4, like *easy*, can either be ascribed to a nominal or to the object of the nominal: a problem is easy to solve or the solution of the problem is easy.

There is a small group of adjectives, comprising *ready*, *eager*, *willing*, and so forth, which lack this ambivalence, in spite of the fact that their attribution to a noun depends upon the presence of a nominal. I shall call them A_6's. Their characteristic occurrences, as in

> He is ready to go
> He is eager to sign the contract

do not have counterparts like

> *To go is ready of him
> *To sign the contract is eager of him.

This feature is sufficient to distingush them from A_5's.

The remaining adjectives, on the contrary, can be attributed to nominals only, and not to nouns. Consider the following examples:

> His death is probable.
> It is necessary that you go away.
> His having won the race is unlikely.

The nominal, obviously, is an imperfect one, and we recognize the typical container adjectives from 5.7. At this point,

[188]

however, I should like to indicate a difference that splits this group into two classes. The first of these is of special interest, since it contains *good* once again. Adjectives belonging to this class may be ascribed to a nominal with the added qualification: *for N*. Some examples:

> It is useful *for me* that you work.
> That you have succeeded is profitable *for us*.
> It is good *for you* that I go away.

Adjectives permitting this kind of relativity will be called A_7's. A_8's, the last class, exclude this move:

> *His arrival is unlikely for us.
> *His death is probable for you.
> *That it is raining is true for us.

Some A_7's are *useful, profitable, pleasant, necessary, good*, and their opposites; some A_8's, *true, false, probable, improbable, likely, certain*, and their contraries.

We said that adjectives belonging to the last three groups are not attributable to simple nouns: there are no unlikely chairs, necessary horses, or probable people. This, of course, does not exclude the possibility of dual, triple, or even quadruple membership: *good*, as we saw, is an A_{3457}. Nor do I want to deny that there are false teeth, impossible people, and necessary evils. An obvious transformational analysis will show, however, that these are elliptical forms and not real counterexamples. Here, as many times before, considerations of length prevent me from working out all the relevant details.

7.8. It is time to collect the pieces belonging to the grammar of the word *good*. The result shows that it fits into four of the eight categories we described: *good* is an A_{3457}.

This means, in the first place, that this adjective enjoys a very great privilege of occurrence indeed; in fact, I cannot think of another of equal versatility. No wonder Ziff thought that this was the reason for its high rank. Yet this is not so. *Unlikely* or *unnecessary*, just to mention a couple of examples, clearly outrank *good*, although their privilege of occurrence is obviously far more limited. In certain cases we might speak of unlikely good results or unnecessary good moves, but hardly of good unlikely results or good unnecessary moves. A_8's outrank any adjective of a lower order regardless of its privilege of occurrence.

Nevertheless *good* remains a high-ranking adjective. It does not occur as an A_1, or A_2.[12] This not only means that it outranks Moore's "natural" properties, but it accounts for its "nonnaturalness," that is, for the impression of remoteness from the subject. *Good* is not a nounlike adjective; it is not tied to the subject directly but, even in the closest case, by means of an appropriate verb. Sentences like

John is good

ring curiously hollow. "Good for what?" one would like to ask, or "You mean that he is a good man?" And then the question still remains: what is a good man?

John is blond

on the other hand, does not create such a vacuous air and raises no further problems.

Going into details, we can say that a person or thing can

---

[12] Phrases like *good for a first novel* might suggest that *good* is sometimes an A_2. We quickly realize, however, that this occurrence is restricted to a relatively small class of noun phrases with a derogatory connotation: one would not say *good for a novel*, unless one meant to imply that novels are by and large not good. Anyway, this fine point (which is due to Sidney S. Shoemaker) is too fine to influence our general conclusions.

be called good on three different grounds. First of all, for what it habitually does or can do ($good_3$). A good dancer is a person who can dance well and habitually dances well, a good king is a monarch who rules or governs his country well, and so forth. Second, something (or somebody) can be called good on the basis of what can be done with it, what it is good for ($good_4$): a good meal is good to eat and a good pen is good for writing. Third, somebody (or something) can be called good because of what he actually does, did, or will do ($good_5$): John may be good to help the poor, and it may be good of Mary to have cooked dinner. Finally, what simply happens, or is the case, may be called good ($good_7$): we often say that it is good that it is raining or that it is good that John has arrived.[13] This much can be gathered immediately from the four transformational models.

7.8.   There are, however, some additional features worth noticing. We mentioned above that in certain ambiguous cases the speaker is expected to supply some added information in order to make his assertion clear. This can occur in situations fitting into (III) and (IV). In both of these frames *good* is predicated of the subject by the intermediary of an appropriate verb class usually determined by a noun. Accordingly, the clarification will consist in providing these elements. Most of the time this is a quite straightforward matter. As we know, a hollow sentence like

John is good

can be neatly fitted into (III) by adding, say,

John is a good dancer

[13] My analysis does not cover occurrences of the type: . . . *tastes* (*looks, smells, feels*) *good*. The narrowness of the relevant verb class will excuse this omission.

or into (IV) by adding

John is a good partner to dance with.

In the first case I supply the noun that immediately suggests the appropriate verb (to dance). In the second, *partner* would not be sufficient by itself; the relevant verb class still remains too large. So I provide a specific verb as well (to dance with somebody). This is like completing the incomprehensible

Venus is a good planet

into

Venus is a good planet to observe.

Yet there remains a significant difference between the two cases. As the last examples show, it is easy to complete the sentence that fits *good* into (IV) even if the noun, by itself, fails to determine the relevant verb class. *Good planet*, unlike, say, *good pen*, is incomprehensible for this reason; planets, unlike pens, have no specific use. Nothing prevents the speaker, however, from specifying the activity, the object of which is the planet, and with respect to which the planet is called good. This happens by adding the verb *to observe*. Moreover, even if the object in question has a specific use, as pens do, the speaker still can qualify that object with respect to a different kind of use, or misuse. An article explorer might say, for example,

This shoe is good to eat.

To put it briefly: things that have no natural use can be put to some use or other, and objects with a natural use still can be put to other uses or misuses. And, accordingly, they can be called good in regard to any of these uses. Language itself recognizes this possibility by leaving the sen-

tence open for the relevant completion: . . . *to V—*.
This is not so with (III). Here, if the noun given is not
sufficient to determine the appropriate verb class, the situation cannot be remedied in any straightforward manner.
This stands to reason. In this case, as we know, *good* quali-
fies the subject with respect to a function denoted by, or
associated with, a noun. This function is discharged by the
subject and not by any other person or thing. The subject
is rated according to what it does and not, as in the previous
case, according to what can be done with it. Therefore, if
the noun given is sterile in this respect—that is to say, if
it fails to indicate a function—the sentence remains obscure
beyond repair. The following examples will illustrate the
rise of this problem:

> John is a good dancer.
> John is a good poet.
> John is a good father.
> John is a good man.
> Fido is a good dog.
> Mumbo is a good baboon.

Dancer gives the verb *to dance* at once. *Good poet* is also
easy to understand: *good* rates John on the basis of one
specific activity, which is writing poetry. The range of
activities on the basis of which John is called good as a
father is much broader, nevertheless still clear enough. As
we jump to Fido, the good dog, the situation becomes
obscure. What is a good dog? We know, more or less,
what makes a good hunting dog, sheep dog, sled dog, and
so forth, but just *good dog* is hardly enough. Of course,
the noun phrases *hunting dog, sheep dog,* and the like denote certain functions, much the same way as *dancer, poet,*
and *father* do. *Dog* alone, however, does not. It makes

sense to say that John is good as a dancer, as a poet, as a father, and it makes sense to say that Fido is good as a hunting dog or sheep dog. On the contrary, it is nonsense to say that Fido is good as a dog. Nevertheless, some intelligibility remains with *good dog;* after all there are some basic requirements that all good dogs (sheep dogs, hunting dogs, and so on) must meet: faithfulness, obedience, and the like, which, as it were, form the common denominator in regard to these functions. In the sad case of Mumbo, the good baboon, we are entirely at a loss: being a baboon is certainly not having a function; moreover, baboons ordinarily are not things that acquire functions, either. What is it that a good baboon is supposed to do well?

Finally we go back to John, the good man. To our surprise, the phrase is understandable. Not only that, but it meets the stronger test as well. We can say that John is not good as a poet, but as a man he is good. To put it in a more obvious way: he is good as a person. The conclusion forces itself upon us: to be a man, to be a person, is like having a function. In our original terminology: the co-occurrences *good—man* or *good—person* must determine an appropriate verb class; that is to say, there must be a set of activities with respect to which somebody can be qualified as good, not as a dancer, poet, or father, but simply as a man.

7.9. At this point, as it often happens in philosophy, we suddenly realize that the path of inquiry we hoped to open is already marked by the footprints of Aristotle.

It is quite clear that the concept of good which Aristotle discusses at the beginning of the *Nicomachean Ethics* corresponds to our $good_3$:

We say "a so-and-so" and a "good so-and-so" have a function which is the same in kind, e.g. a lyre-player and a good lyre-player, and so on without qualification in all cases, eminence in respect of goodness being added to the name of the function (for the function of a lyre-player is to play the lyre, and that of a good lyre-player is to do so well.) [14]

The example of the lyre player, of course, fits into (IIIa), which is the clearest case of (III): the appropriate verb is morphologically obtainable from the noun. But he extends the principle: "The excellence of the eye makes both the eye and its work good; for it is by the excellence of the eye that we see well." [15] Here, too, there is but one appropriate verb determined, though not morphologically, by the noun. This is not necessarily so. Aristotle, in fact, spells out a whole verb class in the next example:

The excellence of the horse makes a horse both good in itself and good at running, and at carrying its rider and at awaiting the attack of the enemy.[16]

(He means, of course, a war horse.) Finally, he applies the same principle to *good man:*

Just as for a flute-player, a sculptor, or any artist, and in general, for all things that have a function or activity, the good and the "well" is thought to reside in the function, so would it seem to be for man, if he has a function. . . . What then can this be? [17]

What is a good man? What is man's function? These questions would lead us far beyond the grammar of the word. Good, no doubt, is good, but this is by no means the end of the matter. Even a complete grammar is only the beginning.

---

[14] 1098a (Oxford Translation). Part of the original is worth quoting: κιθαριστοῦ μὲν γὰρ τὸ κιθαρίζειν, σπουδαίου δὲ τὸ εὖ.
[15] *Ibid.,* 1106a.   [16] *Ibid.*   [17] *Ibid.,* 1097b.

Works Referred To

Alston, W. P. "Philosophical Analysis and Structural Linguistics," *The Journal of Philosophy*, LIX (1962), 709–720.

Anscombe, G. E. M. "On Brute Facts," *Analysis*, XVIII (1957–1958), 69–72.

Aristotle. *Works*, Oxford Translation (eds. J. A. Smith and W. D. Ross). Oxford: Clarendon, 1908–1931.

Austin, J. L. *Philosophical Papers*. Oxford: Clarendon, 1961.

Black, M. *Models and Metaphors: Studies in Language and Philosophy*. Ithaca: Cornell University Press, 1963.

——. "Necessary Statements and Rules," *Philosophical Review*, LXVI (1958), 313–341; reprinted in *Models and Metaphors*.

Boring, E. G., Langfeld, H. S. and Weld, H. P., *Foundations of Psychology*. New York: J. Wiley and Sons, 1948.

Bromberger, S. "An Approach to Explanation," in *Analytical Philosophy*, second series, ed. R. J. Butler. Oxford: Blackwell, 1965.

Butler, R. J., ed. *Analytical Philosophy*. Oxford: Blackwell, 1962.

——, ed. *Analytical Philosophy*, second series. Oxford: Blackwell, 1965.

Carnap, R. *Logical Foundations of Probability*. London: Routledge and Kegan Paul, 1950.

Cavell, S. "Must We Mean What We Say?", *Inquiry*, I (1958), 172–212.

——. "The Availability of Wittgenstein's Later Philosophy," *Philosophical Review*, LXXI (1962), 67–93.

WORKS REFERRED TO

Chomsky, N. *Syntactic Structures*. 'S-Gravenhage: Mouton and Co., 1957.

Dubs, H. H. "Language and Philosophy," *Philosophical Review*, LXIV (1958), 437.

Edwards, P., ed. *Encyclopedia of Philosophy*. New York: Macmillan, 1967.

Findlay, J. N. "Use, Usage and Meaning," *Proceedings of the Aristotelian Society*, supp. vol. XXV (1961), 231–242.

Fodor, J. A. and Katz, J. J. "The Availability of What We Say," *Philosophical Review*, LXXII (1963), 57–71.

——, eds. *The Structure of Language: Readings in the Philosophy of Language*. Englewood Cliffs: Prentice-Hall, 1964.

——. "The Structure of Semantic Theory," in *The Structure of Language*, pp. 473–518.

——. "What Is Wrong with the Philosophy of Language?" *Inquiry*, V (1962), 197–237.

Geach, P. T., "Good and Evil," *Analysis*, XVII (1956), 33–42.

Goodman, N. *The Structure of Appearance*. Cambridge, Mass.: Harvard University Press, 1951.

Hare, R. M. "Are Discoveries about the Uses of Words Empirical?" *Journal of Philosophy*, LIV (1957), 741–750.

Harris, Z. S. "Co-occurrence and Transformation in Linguistic Structure," *Language* 33 (1957), 283–340.

——. *String Analysis of Sentence Structure* (Papers on Formal Linguistics, No. 1). The Hague: Mouton and Co., 1962.

——. "Transformational Theory," *Language* 41 (1965), 363–401.

Hiż, H. "Congrammaticality, Batteries of Transformations, and Grammatical Categories," *Proceedings of the Symposia in Applied Mathematics*, American Mathematical Society, 12 (1961), 43–50.

Hume, D. *A Treatise of Human Nature*, ed. L. A. Selby-Bigge. Oxford: Clarendon, 1888.

Kant, I. *Critique of Pure Reason*, trans. N. Kemp Smith. London: Macmillan, 1953.

——. *Prolegomena*, in *Kant's Gesammelte Schriften*, Hrsg. von der königlich Preussischen Akademie der Wissenschaften, Band IV. Berlin: G. Reimer, 1911.

Katz, J. J. *The Philosophy of Language*. New York and London: Harper & Row, 1966.

Lees, R. B. *The Grammar of English Nominalizations*, Supplement to *International Journal of American Linguistics*, 26 (1960).

WORKS REFERRED TO

Locke, J. *An Essay Concerning Human Understanding*, ed. A. C. Fraser. New York: Dover, 1959.

Moore, G. E. *Principia Ethica*. Cambridge: Cambridge University Press, 1903.

Nicod, J. *Foundations of Geometry and Induction*. London: Routledge & Kegan Paul, 1930.

Quine, W. V. *Mathematical Logic*, rev. ed. Cambridge, Mass.: Harvard University Press, 1951.

——. *Methods of Logic*, rev. ed. New York: Holt, Rinehart and Winston, 1964.

Robbins, B. *The Transformational Status of the Definite Article in English* (Papers on Formal Linguistics, No. 4). The Hague–Paris: Mouton, in preparation.

Russell, B. *Introduction to Mathematical Philosophy*. London: Allen and Unwin, 1920.

Ryle, G. *The Concept of Mind*. New York: Barnes and Noble, 1949.

——. *Dilemmas*. Cambridge: Cambridge University Press, 1954.

——. "Ordinary Language," *Philosophical Review*, LXII (1953), 167–186.

——. "Use, Usage and Meaning," *Proceedings of the Aristotelian Society*, supp. vol. XXV (1961), pp. 223–230.

Shorter, J. M. "Causality and a Method of Analysis" in *Analytical Philosophy*, second series, ed. R. J. Butler. pp. 145–157.

Sibley, F. N. "Seeking, Scrutinizing and Seeing," *Mind*, LXIV (1955), 455–478.

Strawson, P. F. *Individuals: an Essay in Descriptive Metaphysics*, London: Methuen and Co., 1959.

——. "On Referring," *Mind*, LIX (1950), 320–344.

Tsu-Lin Mei. "Subject and Predicate, a Grammatical Preliminary," *Philosophical Review*, LXX (1961), 153–175.

Vendler, Z. *Adjectives and Nominalizations* (Papers on Formal Linguistics, No. 5). The Hague–Paris: Mouton, 1968.

Whorf, B. L. *Language, Thought and Reality: Selected Writings of Benjamin Lee Whorf*, ed. J. B. Caroll. Cambridge, Mass.: Technology Press, 1956.

Wittgenstein, L. *Philosophical Investigations*. Oxford: Blackwell, 1953.

——. *Tractatus Logico-Philosophicus*. London: Routledge & Kegan Paul, 1922.

Ziff, P. *Semantic Analysis*. Ithaca: Cornell University Press, 1960.

Index

[201]